RETHINKING REFORM:

The Principal's Dilemma

A Special Report of the NASSP Curriculum Council

Herbert J. Walberg
James W. Keefe
Editors

NATIONAL ASSOCIATION OF SECONDARY SCHOOL PRINCIPALS
1904 Association Drive, Reston, Virginia 22091

Contributors

Fenwick W. English, Professor of Education, Lehigh University, Bethlehem, Pennsylvania

Allan A. Glatthorn, Graduate School of Education, University of Pennsylvania, Philadelphia

James W. Keefe, NASSP Director of Research, Reston, Virginia

Jane Stallings, Professor and Chair, Department of Curriculum and Instruction, University of Houston, Texas

Daniel Tanner, Professor of Education, Rutgers University, New Brunswick, New Jersey

Herbert J. Walberg, Professor of Human Development and Learning and Research Professor of Education, University of Illinois at Chicago Circle.

NASSP

Scott D. Thomson, Executive Director

Thomas F. Koerner, Editor and Director of Publications

Eugenia C. Potter, Technical Editor

Copyright 1986 by NASSP
All Rights Reserved
ISBN 0882101935

National Association of Secondary School Principals
1904 Association Drive
Reston, Virginia 22091
(703) 860-0200

Contents

Foreword

The National Association of Secondary School Principals' charter commits the Association to pursue activities for the improvement of secondary education. Since its inception, the NASSP has undertaken many types of research and service activities as well as large-scale projects. In recent years, Association activity has moved more and more to instructional issues and school improvement as a complement to the traditional school management agenda.

In May 1985, NASSP's Board of Directors approved the establishment of a Curriculum Council to assist the Association in developing and implementing a systematic agenda in curriculum and instruction. The Council will act as the research and development arm of NASSP's national Curriculum Committee.

Five scholars with differing perspectives on curriculum development and educational improvement were invited to form the initial Council. The members of the Council are Allan Glatthorn, Council chair, Fenwick English, Jane Stallings, Daniel Tanner, and Herbert Walberg. James Keefe works with the Council as NASSP staff representative.

The Council, as its first order of business, agreed to prepare a special report that would speak to the dilemmas posed for principals and other educators by the recent educational reform reports. The report would provide principals with a constructive tool for analyzing and acting upon the recommendations of the reform studies. The editors hope that this document serves that worthwhile purpose.

H.J.W.
J.W.K.

CHAPTER 1

Introduction: What Dilemmas?

James W. Keefe

PRINCIPALS KNOW ABOUT DILEMMAS. THEY MAKE CAREERS of solving difficult problems involving equally undesirable alternatives. But even those who daily must sort out perplexing choices can find school reform confusing. Regrettably, neither teachers nor principals are consulted when reform reports are debated; educators, in fact, are the object of reform. In some respects, they deserve the limelight because schools have been slow to make systematic changes. Specifically, little progress has been made toward the structural changes that support the personalization of teaching and learning. Most educators prefer the system as it is.

Reluctance to change notwithstanding, educators face various dilemmas when blue ribbon committees attempt to reform schooling. Reformers reflect differing philosophical traditions, various levels of educational sophistication, and greater or lesser empathy with the real problems of operating schools. As a result, educational reforms become as much a passing fad as federal programs for this or that target group. When reform becomes fad, dilemmas abound.

Principals in particular are faced with a continuing series of conundrums. No matter what cause they champion, the debate never ends. It reminds one of G. H. Reavis' (1956) illustration of the Animal School.

> Once upon a time, the animals decided they must do something heroic to meet the problems of a "new world." So they organized a school.
>
> They adopted an activity curriculum consisting of running, climbing, swimming, and flying. To make it easier to administer the curriculum, all the animals took all the subjects.
>
> The duck was excellent in swimming, in fact better than his instructor; but he made only passing grades in flying and was very poor in running. Since he was slow in running, he had to stay after school and also drop swimming in order to practice running. This was kept up until his web feet were badly worn and he was only average in swimming. But average was acceptable in school, so nobody worried about that except the duck.
>
> The rabbit started at the top of the class in running, but had a nervous breakdown because of so much make-up work in swimming.

The squirrel was excellent in climbing until he developed frustration in the flying class where his teacher made him start from the ground up instead of from the treetop down. He also developed "charlie horses" from over-exertion and then got a "C" in climbing and a "D" in running.

The eagle was a problem child and was disciplined severely. In the climbing class he beat all the others to the top of the tree, but insisted on using his own way of getting there.

At the end of the year, an abnormal eel that could swim exceedingly well, and also run, climb, and fly a little had the highest average and was valedictorian.

The prairie dogs stayed out of school and fought the tax levy because the administration would not add digging and burrowing to the curriculum. They apprenticed their child to a badger and later joined the groundhogs and gophers to start a successful private school.

Principals and schools face a lot of prairie dogs and badgers these days.

Can principals surmount the dilemmas of educational reform? Yes, but only by identifying and confronting the dilemmas, by exerting educational leadership even in the face of all the confusion.

The dilemmas of leadership are many, but some stand out.

- Are school reform movements like a swinging pendulum? Are countermovements for academic excellence and humanizing the schools reconcilable? What about the place of the comprehensive high school in an increasingly competitive environment? What is the role of the principal as educational or instructional leader? How can schools engage in real educational reconstruction?
- Is reform really needed? Are the reform reports valid? What do changes in the work environment, in science and technology, and in the family imply for schooling?
- What does it mean to be "in charge" of the school curriculum? Can schools really change? Does instructional improvement strengthen the curriculum? Has curricular control drifted from the building to district and state levels? What do principals who exercise control do?
- How do principals find the time for educational leadership? How can principals surmount recurring crises? What about the administrative team approach? How can the staff be systematically involved in school improvement? What organizational structures extend the influence of the principal in program development and improvement?
- What effect will curricular reform have on students at risk? Will more academics, more time, and more rigorous promotional standards help or hurt high-risk students? What alternative approaches are available?
- Should schools cut the curriculum? What decisions influence balance in the curriculum? How can schools achieve curricular integration? What about the cocurriculum?
- How does the school schedule affect the curriculum? How should subject area and instructional time be allocated? How can principals help teachers improve their curriculum-making skills? What about

zine article titled "Technology Is Knocking at the Schoolhouse Door." Now "the remaking of American education" was to come from the British open classroom, by which our schools would become "humanized."

As the open-classroom movement was making a mark on our elementary schools, U.S. Commissioner of Education Sidney Marland launched a national program for career education. "We must purge ourselves of academic snobbery," declared Marland, as he criticized our schools and society for placing excessive emphasis on going to college (Marland, 1971).

Marland's program for career education was announced less than a year after the report issued by President Nixon's Commission on Campus Unrest (1970). Ironically, Marland did not stay to implement his program; soon after, he accepted the presidency of the College Entrance Examination Board.

Counterreaction: Educational Retrenchment

The excessive efforts to humanize the school during the late '60s and early '70s were met by an educational retrenchment through "back-to-basics." The era of retrenchment was aided and abetted by university researchers who looked to the limits, rather than the possibilities, of schooling.

One of the baffling aspects of research on the effects of formal education is the tendency for university researchers to evaluate schooling negatively, whereas they invariably find positive results when studying higher education. How is it that schools can make little difference while colleges make such a difference in people's lives?

Everything we know about human growth and development reveals that if the effects of higher education are positive, powerful, and pervasive, the effects of elementary and secondary education should be even more positive, powerful, and pervasive.

Gunnar Myrdal (1969) observed to his dismay that the great tradition in social science that championed the cause of popular education was, in recent years, being abandoned. Many university scholars have a vested interest in advancing their own case and see the schools as competitors for educational funding. They seem to have adopted an elitist stance toward the secondary school. And, of course, in social research it is far easier to find negative rather than positive outcomes.

This situation has led to a profound negativism toward the schools by university scholars who would do well to heed the dictum of the late Robert Benchley that, "You can't prove that platypuses don't lay eggs by photographing platypuses not laying eggs." Yet this is precisely what the university researchers seem to do when the instruments they use in their research on the effects of schooling fail to account for over 60 percent of the variance (Jencks et al., 1973).

This negativism of university scholars toward the schools reflected and gave impetus to the climate of sociopolitical conservatism and the retrenchment of "back-to-basics" during the 1970s. A series of reports issued on the adolescent and the secondary school during the '70s portrayed adolescence as a pathological stage in human development.

The situation was regarded as so severe and pervasive that it prompted the U.S. Science Advisory Committee to form a Panel on Youth to study the ways of eliminating our nation's "youth problem." The panel's solution was to shorten or accelerate the transition to adulthood for the non-college-bound. The college-bound could continue to develop in high school, whereas the "others" would be shunted out of school and into other vehicles of preparation for the world of work (Coleman, 1974).

Also issued during this time were the report of the National Commission on the Reform of Secondary Education, sponsored by the Kettering Foundation (1973), and the report on the National Panel on High School and Adolescent Education, under the auspices of the U.S. Office of Education (1976).

All these reports viewed the problem of youth disaffection, unemployment, and disruption as evidence that our schools had failed and that it was time to return the high school to its narrow academic mission by emphasizing basic academic skills. This retrenchment was to be followed by work training and education in nonschool settings for the masses, and a higher-order academic program in the high school for the college-bound.

In essence, the reports called for the elimination of the comprehensive high school in favor of an academic high school, the creation of alternative schools for youngsters who did not fit into the academic setting, emphasis on the mastery of basic skills, reduction in the age of compulsory school attendance and in the length of the school day, the allocation of public funds to businesses and industries to support the training of adolescents for work, and other alternatives to schooling for the masses.

The comprehensive high school was conceived early in this century as the vehicle for bringing together youths from different backgrounds and destinations, and for serving their common and diversified needs through a comprehensive curriculum.

The panels and commissions of the 1970s, however, regarded this heterogeneous mix in the comprehensive high school as serving only to call attention to social differences. Apparently, by segregating adolescents from one another according to differences in their social origins and destinations, they would be spared the unsettling task of learning how to work out their differences.

The great vision of creating unity from diversity, a vision that had long served as the ideal of American democracy and of its unique institution—the comprehensive high school—was to be abandoned for fear that mixing students from different backgrounds in the comprehensive high school would merely affirm that, although all are created equal, some are more equal than others. James Conant was no longer on the scene to defend the comprehensive high school, and the education profession made no concerted effort to support this unique institution. A dual educational system appeared to be in the making through the creation of segregated, specialized area or county vocational schools. Such schools were being established in this country at a time when other advanced democratic nations were adopting the comprehensive model.

At the same time, our states were embarking on minimum competency testing and reducing the school curriculum to the lowest common denominator of basic skills. (Writing, for example, could not be subjected to quantifiable measures, so it was not included in these tests.) By the late 1970s and early 1980s, the National Assessment of Educational Progress (NAEP) had discovered declines in student abilities to think and to apply their knowledge. NAEP attributed these declines to the back-to-basics retrenchment and statewide minimum competency testing. Nobody remembered the efforts by experimentalist progressive educators who, over several decades, had struggled to make reflective thinking the underlying theme of the curriculum. A wave of censorship of schoolbooks and other curricular materials began once again. Error-oriented teaching dominated the scene; idea-oriented teaching was regarded as risky and inefficient.

The 1983 *New York Times Survey of Education* featured the theme, "Teaching To Think: A New Emphasis," forgetting that teaching to think was an emphasis promulgated by John Dewey early in this century. Nevertheless, the "new emphasis" on teaching to think was being treated as a special skill to be injected into the curriculum as a separate component. Schools made few concerted efforts to reconstruct the curriculum in general education to reemphasize reflective thinking on the pervasive and disturbing problems of youth and of the wider society.

The New National Crisis and the Pursuit of Academic Excellence

In 1983, in the wake of the Japanese assault on our world industrial and technological markets, the National Science Board of the National Science Foundation proposed a multi-billion dollar investment to revamp the school curriculum in science, mathematics, and technology.

The report of the National Science Board held that precedent for such federal involvement had been well established when our nation needed "an urgent program to produce vital talent . . . in wartime or the national response to Sputnik" (p. 65). "The National Science Foundation, which has recognized expertise in leading curriculum development should again take the leadership role in promoting curriculum evaluation and development for mathematics, science and technology" (p. xi). (Remember, this group gave us the new math and the new science during the period of perceived crisis in national security during the '50s and '60s.)

Also appearing in 1983 was the report, *A Nation at Risk*, issued by the National Commission on Excellence at the behest of the U.S. Secretary of Education. This report declared that, "The citizen is dismayed at a steady 15-year decline in industrial productivity as one great American industry after another falls to world competition" (p. 18). It blamed our schools for this latest crisis. "If an unfriendly foreign power had attempted to impose on America the mediocre educational performance that exists today, we might well have viewed it as an act of war," the Commission stated in the opening page of its report.

The Commission alleged (p. 8) that our schools failed to measure up to those of other nations on international comparisons of student achievement. The Commission neglected to acknowledge that these comparisons were based on test scores representing only 8 to 14 percent of the secondary school age population of most of the nations in the study, in contrast to our 70 percent. It also failed to acknowledge that the United States led all other nations in educational yield. Not until page 34 of the 36-page report did the Commission acknowledge that our top students actually "compared favorably in achievement with their peers in other countries." Similar distortions are in evidence in the report of the National Science Board on these international comparisons of educational achievement (p. 17).

Although the National Commission on Excellence had been explicitly charged with assessing the quality of our nation's colleges and universities as well as our schools, no such assessment was made of higher education. Apparently, the Commission's membership, which was chaired by a university president and which included several other university presidents or former presidents, chose not to throw stones at their own houses.

The call for vastly expanded federal financing of public education appeared at a time when the policy of the Executive branch of our federal government was geared to the reduction of federal support for public education.

The Secretary of Education found himself in an awkward position. Yet, within seven months of the appearance of *A Nation at Risk*, the staff of the Commission issued a report at the behest of the Secretary titled *Meeting the Challenge* (November 15, 1983). This report opened with the following words: "Throughout the nation, public and private actions by individuals and groups at local, state, and national levels are meeting the challenge to improve education. . . . *A Nation at Risk* has had a remarkable impact . . . since its publication on April 26, 1983."

Schools apparently had undergone a remarkable transformation from disastrous decline to veritable renaissance. And all this without any federal infusion of dollars. Never before in our history had so much been done so fast with so little. Initiatives by the individual states were effecting the needed cure.

The more immediate impact of the various reform reports of the 1980s has been for the states to increase the years of required study of certain academic courses for high school graduation. Unfortunately, these requirements do nothing to meet the need for a coherent curriculum of general education and diversified studies.

The Principal as Educational Leader

In contrast to most other school reform reports, the studies by Ernest Boyer and John Goodlad issued in 1983 seem to be more carefully considered and balanced. Yet, certain prescriptions by Boyer and Goodlad are disturbing.

In a chapter titled "Classrooms and Corporations," Boyer holds that in the schools, "business and industry also can be administrators, particularly in aiding principals in their capacity as manager and leader." In my perception, too much has been made of casting the school principal as a managerial rather than educational leader.

School principals must be educational leaders and not mere managers. At the 1968 Annual Conference of the NASSP, an officer of the Ford Foundation likened the principal to the industrial plant manager, and described the school in these words: "the school, like an industrial plant, represents a process. Raw material goes in and a product comes out" (Meade).

The current literature on educational reform continues to cast the principal in the role of plant manager. Yet anyone engaged in the education of children and youth knows that they cannot be likened to raw materials to be fashioned into finished products like canned hams and VCRs.

As an educational leader, the principal must convey to the staff of the school a sense of vision about human potential and work with the staff and students to open the paths to these possibilities. In the human equation, outcomes cannot be guaranteed. As Woodrow Wilson, then president of Princeton, told a concerned mother who was badgering him over the care that would be taken of her son, soon to enter the university as a freshman: "Madame, we guarantee the results, or we cheerfully return the boy."

Boyer and Goodlad wisely recognize the need for a coherent curriculum in general education or common learnings in the high school (even though one may take issue with their curricular prescriptions), but both authors choose only to look to the limitations rather than the possibilities of vocational studies in the high school.

Under their proposals, the comprehensive high school would be eliminated in favor of a general academic high school. Yet no advanced industrial nation can do without vocational education. The question is whether it will be provided within the unitary structure of the comprehensive high school or through a divided school system—as in the class-divided European nations.

Unless our comprehensive high schools are strengthened, the present trend toward a divided school system will become an accomplished fact, and adolescents will be divided from one another according to background and destination. Too many educators today are willing to abandon this uniquely

American invention which has produced universal secondary education, open-access higher education, and the highest educational yield of any nation on earth.

The Way Out of the Confusion

"Ours is the age of crisis," declares Charles Silberman in the opening words of *Crisis in the Classroom*. "Our nation is at risk," declaims the opening sentence of the report of the National Commission on Excellence in Education. "American schools are in trouble," writes John Goodlad in the opening sentence of *A Place Called School*. "Education is in the headlines once again," states Ernest Boyer in the opening sentence of *High School: A Report on Secondary Education in America*.

Our schools seem to be in a perpetual state of crisis. The conflicting and contradictory prescriptions offered in successive eras by so many external agencies and individual critics tend to leave any thoughtful educator in a state of frustration and confusion. One alternative is to find the direction of the dominant tide at any given time and ride it for all it is worth. This strategy gives the appearance of great movement, although it produces little or no progress. In fact, it is invariably counterproductive because one must always be prepared for a shift in the opposite direction.

The way out of the confusion is to begin resolving the false antitheses that move us from narrow-minded prescriptions to narrow-minded antidotes and back again. Mark Twain satirized the cyclical phenomenon of social reform and retrenchment as "Twain's Law of Periodical Repetition."

Dewey (1904) addressed this same problem early in this century when he observed that we must break the chain of successive reforms by reaction and counterreaction in which each reform is undertaken to undo the excesses of its predecessor and, in turn, creates excesses of its own. Dewey was not making a plea for moderation or for striking a balance between opposing points. When each opposing side is wrong, the middle point does not become the right one.

Consider the pendulum. Those who see the correct position as a midpoint balance between swings to the two extremes should recognize that the pendulum stops at the midpoint only when the clock stops working. Even when the pendulum is swinging, time is passing. Generations are going through school, exposed to whatever fad happens to be dominant in their time.

In fact, the swinging pendulum in physics represents very nearly a simple harmonic motion. In our changing movements of school reform and counterreform, the motion is anything but harmonic. There are great collisions and misdirections, resulting in great losses of energy. How do we recoup this energy and prevent its loss in the future?

Dewey held that solution comes by getting away from the opposing opinions and by attacking the problem with a fresh light. This approach requires considerable thought, for it is far easier to see things separately. Dewey was addressing the opposition between child-centered and subject-centered advocates—a problem that continues to this day because one falsely assumes that an advantage for one side must be taken at the expense of the other side. The child is placed in opposition to the curriculum, a position that is untenable for education (Dewey, 1902).

Today, we have established a similar series of falsely dichotomous priorities:

- The gifted and talented must be served at the expense of others
- The disadvantaged must be served at the expense of the gifted and talented
- Priority must be given to the sciences and mathematics at the expense of the arts and humanities
- The academic subjects must come above and in opposition to the vocational subjects
- College-bound students must be served above the others
- The basics must come first and above all else in the curriculum
- Standards must be raised even if more students must fail or drop out of school
- Educational quality must be secured at the expense of quantity
- Discipline must be achieved at the expense of freedom
- Individuality must be advanced at the expense of social responsibility
- Social responsibility must wipe out individuality
- The cultivation of the intellect must come at the expense of the cultivation of the person
- Cognitive learning must precede and prevail over affective learning
- Cultural subjects must hold sway over practical studies; and so on.

"Common sense recoils at the extreme character of the results" of such false oppositions; yet these oppositions prevail (Dewey, 1902, p. 10).

The great quandary faced by school administrators is their commitment to be responsive to the public. Administrators are under great political pressure to demonstrate their responsiveness by submitting to whatever external forces are dominant at any particular time.

Politicians and special-interest groups can act opportunistically in attacking the schools and in promoting simplistic remedies for complex educational problems. Politicians do not have to live with the consequences of their remedies, antidotes, or panaceas; school administrators and teachers are left to face the consequences of reaction and counterreaction.

The way out of the quandary for school administrators is to remember that responsiveness to the public does not mean capitulation to whatever external force is dominant at any particular time. Responsiveness means responsibility—protecting and advancing the best interests of the rising generation. Responsiveness lies in commitment to educational improvement, to seeking and applying the best available evidence in solving problems.

Reform proposals must be evaluated carefully and collegially by school administrators and their professional staffs.

In undertaking such evaluations, they might ask:

- Was the reform proposal tried before?
- What happened?
- What can we learn from the educational record (past experience) of similar reform efforts?
- Are there any indications that the proposed reforms will occur at the expense of other desirable educational measures or practices?
- Do the reform measures claim advantages for any special student population that can take place only at the expense of another population?
- Do the reforms run counter to our best available educational knowledge?
- Are the reforms consonant with what we know about the nature of the developing learner (child or adolescent)?
- Are the reforms in harmony with our widest social interest as a democracy?
- Is the professional staff committed to the proposed reform measures?

Reform measures imposed on teachers cannot be successful. The result of imposition by authority or mandate is overt compliance and covert resistance. By unleashing the teacher's intelligence, we can avoid incessant cycles of fads and fashions, of shortsighted remedies followed by emergency antidotes.

Addressing this problem in 1904, Dewey wrote, "The tendency of educational development to proceed by reaction from one thing to another, to adopt for one year, or for a term of seven years, this or that new study or method of teaching, and then as abruptly to swing over to some new educational gospel, is a result which would be impossible if teachers were adequately moved by their own intelligence" (p. 16).

A recent notable example of statesmanlike responsiveness was the action in the fall of 1985 by the California Board of Education, under the leadership of Superintendent Bill Honig, in following the recommendations of a statewide curriculum committee to reject every science textbook for seventh and eighth grades because the texts had watered down the treatment of evolution to avoid controversy.

In putting a dunce cap on some 30 textbooks, Superintendent Honig was quoted as saying, "The issue here is, are we going to allow publishers to water down texts and draft them politically to avoid controversy? Doing so undermines our efforts toward excellence in our classrooms" (*The New York Times*, Sept. 14, 1985, p. 1). Honig went on to stress that the board would also reject inadequate textbooks in other fields such as history and social studies which gloss over controversial issues. Superintendent Honig was acting as an educational leader for his board of education.

Superintendents and principals at the local level can learn a lesson from the events in California. As educational leaders, they have a responsibility for educating their boards as well as their professional staffs, parents, and the public about educational needs and accomplishments. Administrators need not be blown by whatever ill wind may be dominant at a given time.

The way out of our current confusion is to reconstruct education so that the curriculum, the learner, and our highest and widest social aims are ordered in vital, harmonic interdependence.

A free society requires a citizenry capable of reflective or independent thinking in the context of shared social responsibility. The counterreaction of "back-to-basics" during the late '70s and early '80s severed skills from ideas. Minimum competencies mean a curriculum reduced to the lowest common denominator. The nature of the learner and our highest and widest social aims are neglected and undermined if we revert to a nineteenth-century conception of schooling for the masses—schooling limited to basic education and fundamental literacy.

The contemporary call to mobilize the schools to meet the economic interests of global competition suffers from the same weaknesses and contradictions as the 1950s mobilization of the schools for the Cold War and space race. If nationalism is allowed to prevail over cosmopolitanism, if the individual and the emerging generation are to be made subordinate to narrow and immediate economic interests, our society will not be true to itself.

We must give recognition to the very real accomplishments of our unitary and comprehensive public school structure, which has resulted in the greatest educational yield and the lowest social bias of any nation on earth. Since midcentury, the United States has been universally recognized for its dominant position in leading mathematical and science journals, in international prizes for the advancement of knowledge, and in scientific patents. None of this would be possible without an effective system of public education. If we have slipped in our dominance over global industrial markets, we cannot solve the problem by making our schools the scapegoat.

Not since the demise of the Educational Policies Commission almost 20 years ago has there been a completely nonpartisan body to speak out for American public education. Established in 1936 with funds from the NEA, the Educational Policies Commission served for four decades as an independent body to examine American educational policy in the light of our nation's democratic ideas.

Having no axe to grind, the Commission spoke out courageously and with great vision for universal secondary education; for a unitary, rather than a divided school structure; for the existence of general education, college preparatory studies, and vocational education in mutual enhancement in the comprehensive high school; for the extension of educational opportunity for all; for the development of open-access higher education through the community college and the state university; for the promotion of the health and well-being of the disadvantaged and disaffected; for the secular school in a polyglot society.

Quite remarkably, despite the diverse backgrounds and viewpoints of the membership over these decades, the Commission was able to share a common faith and vision. In his autobiography, Conant describes his own education about American public education as a result of serving as a member and chairman of the Educational Policies Commission on and off for 22 years.

Not one of our existing professional educational associations has been able to fill the vacuum left by the demise of the Commission. Instead, special-interest groups have tended to fill the vacuum. Perhaps the various professional associations in education should jointly create a continuing fund for the re-creation of an independent and permanent Educational Policies Commission.

Many leading educators over the years have echoed the truism that schools must reflect society. Unfortunately, too many persons take this to mean that schools are powerless to do more than they are doing. They fail to recognize that schools can seek to reflect the best in society, not the worst. Fundamentally this is the expectation that the public holds for its schools. Any other vision is narrow and destructive. No other vision can stop the pendulum swings, resolve the false antitheses, and bring our actions into harmony with our highest ideals.

References

American Institute of Physics. *Physics in Your High School*. New York: McGraw-Hill, 1960.

Astin, A. W. *Four Critical Years*. San Francisco, Calif.: Jossey-Bass, 1977.

Boyer, E. L. *High School*. New York: Harper & Row, 1983.

Bruner, J.S. *The Process of Education*. Cambridge, Mass.: Harvard University Press, 1960.

Coleman, J.S., and others. *Youth: Transition to Adulthood. Report of the Panel on Youth of the President's Science Advisory Committee*. Chicago, Ill.: University of Chicago Press, 1974.

Conant, J. B. *The American High School*. New York: McGraw-Hill, 1959.

———. *My Several Lives*. New York: Harper & Row, 1970.

Dewey, J. *The Child and the Curriculum*. Chicago, Ill.: University of Chicago Press, 1902.

———. *How We Think*. Lexington, Mass.: D. C. Heath, 1933.

———. "The Relation of Theory to Practice in Education." In *The Relation of Theory to Practice in the Education of Teachers*, Third Yearbook of the National Society for the Scientific Study of Education, Part I. Bloomington, Ill.: Public School Publishing Co., 1904.

Ellis, S.D. "Enrollment Trends." *Physics Today* 20(1967):77.

Goodlad, J. I. *A Place Called School*. New York: McGraw-Hill, 1983.

Hall, E. "Bad Education—A Conversation with Jerome Bruner." *Psychology Today* 4(1970):51.

Husén, T. "Are Standards in U.S. Schools Really Lagging Behind Those in Other Countries?" *Phi Delta Kappan* 64(1983):455-461.

Jencks, C., et al. *Inequality.* New York: Basic Books, 1972.

King, L.C. "High Student Failure Rate Serious Problem." *Chemical and Engineering News* 45(1967):44.

Marland, S. P., Jr. "Career Education Now." Address at the Annual Convention of the National Association of Secondary School Principals, Houston, Texas, January 23, 1971.

Meade, E. J., Jr. "Accountability and Governance in Public Education." New York: Ford Foundation, 1968.

Myrdal, G. *Objectivity in Social Research.* New York: Pantheon Books, 1969.

National Assessment of Educational Progress. *Reading, Science, and Mathematics Trends.* Denver: NAEP, 1983.

National Commission on Excellence in Education. *A Nation at Risk.* Washington, D.C.: U.S. Department of Education, 1983.

National Commission on the Reform of Secondary Education. *The Reform of Secondary Education.* New York: McGraw-Hill, 1973.

National Panel on High School and Adolescent Education. *The Education of Adolescents.* Washington, D.C.: U.S. Office of Education, 1976.

National Science Board. *Educating Americans for the 21st Century.* Washington, D.C.: National Science Foundation, 1983.

The New York Times Survey of Education. "Teaching to Think: A New Emphasis." January, 1983.

Report of the Harvard Committee. *General Education in a Free Society.* Cambridge, Mass.: Harvard University Press, 1945.

Report of the President's Commission on Campus Unrest. *Campus Unrest.* Washington, D.C.: U.S. Government Printing Office, 1970.

Report to the Secretary of Education. *Meeting the Challenge.* Washington, D.C.: U.S. Department of Education, 1983.

Rickover, H. G. *American Education: A National Failure.* New York: Dutton, 1959.

Silberman, C. E. (1970). *Crisis in the Classroom.* New York: Random House, 1970.

———. "Technology Is Knocking at the Schoolhouse Door." *Fortune* 74(1966):122.

Stanley, P. W. Remarks at the Annual Meeting of the Association of Governing Boards of Universities and Colleges, Miami Beach, Fla., April, 1985.

Watley, D. J., and Nichols, R. C. *Career Decisions of Talented Youth.* Evanston, Ill.: National Merit Scholarship Corp., 1969.

CHAPTER 3

Are Reforms Really Needed?

Herbert J. Walberg

T HE MID-1980s ARE A TIME OF UNPRECEDENTED curriculum ferment and educational reform. As indicated in the previous section, the National Commission on Excellence in Education's report to the U.S. Secretary of Education, *A Nation at Risk,* began a series of reports that brought new facts, insights, and pressures upon educators.

Interestingly, the reports were written largely by those outside the public schools. The authors included scholars from higher education, business people, governors, legislators, scientists, and others. They purported to represent the student and the national interest rather than the interests of professional educators. They called upon educators to do more than they had done in the past, to change the curriculum, and to increase their productivity.

The national reports gained considerable publicity. The mass media featured them; and the authors spoke to large audiences and debated one another at meetings throughout the country. *A Nation at Risk* was translated into many languages, and an estimated 600,000 copies were reproduced. By 1985, state legislatures had appointed several hundred commissions and committees to recommend new educational legislation.

The reports pointed to achievement test comparisons of U.S. students with those in other countries, and of current students with those of a decade or more ago. The apparent declines on the Scholastic Aptitude Test, taken by college applicants, were most often cited. Although such comparisons are complicated and possibly misleading, some appeared alarming. Poor achievement would not only hurt students themselves but also reduce further the efficiency of colleges, industry, and the military that all devote money, time, and energy to remedial work.

The reports also pointed to the importance of "time on task." They noted that American classes run about 180 days per year in contrast to longer school years in other countries, notably 240 days in Japan, a country that often led in achievement test comparisons (Walberg, 1983).

If time was the cause of educational shortcomings in terms of measured results, then the outcomes to be feared would be a workforce without knowledge and a future without prosperity. This argument goes back at least two centuries to Adam Smith's *Wealth of Nations,* which held that welfare depends not only upon physical and financial capital but also upon the abilities of people, or "human capital."

Evaluations of the Reports

We will not assess the assertions put forward in the reports nor evaluate their many recommendations. The reports are voluminous and number in the dozens. Moreover, commentary is available elsewhere.

From a curriculum standpoint, for example, Tanner (1984a, 1984b) criticized *A Nation at Risk*, Ernest Boyer's Carnegie Foundation report, the Education Commission of the States' *Action for Excellence, Educating for the 21st Century*, Mortimer Adler's *The Paideia Proposal*, John Goodlad's *A Place Called School*, and Theodore Sizer's *Horace's Compromise*. Writing for *The Brookings Review*, Peterson (1983) also found the reports disappointing. He felt they lacked a "focused statement of the problem to be analyzed, methodical evaluation of existing research, reasoned consideration of the options, and presentation of supporting evidence and argumentation for well-specified proposals" (p. 3).

Walberg (1983), on the other hand, looked favorably on the reports. He reviewed the facts and causal assertions about instructional time and quality, test scores, and economic growth, and concluded that making schools more productive would contribute to the national welfare. The Board of Directors of the National Association of Secondary School Principals (1983) put forward a *Statement on National Reports* that supported several of the major recommendations. Our concern, however, is not with the detailed substance and evaluation of the reports, but with their implications for schools.

The Impact and Context of the Reform Reports

The reports and discussions of them had quick, substantial, and widespread effects. According to Odden (1986, p. 335):

> The education reform movement has moved faster than any public policy reform in modern history. All the states have expanded their school improvement programs, nearly all have increased high school graduation requirements, most have stiffened college admission requirements, many are deepening the content of course offerings, and many are enacting a variety of policies to strengthen the teaching profession.

It should be obvious that whether or not the reports are accurate about the facts and wise in their recommendations, they are having an enormous impact on schools—particularly through the activities of governors and state legislatures. It is worth remembering that the U.S. Constitution leaves education to the states; and it is the citizens or their representatives in the legislatures and on school boards that shoulder the ultimate responsibility for educational policy and finance of public schools.

Education and educational reform take place not in a vacuum but in the context of society and particular social institutions. Hurd (1986, p. 356) points out, "public pressure for immediate action and visible results overwhelm the major issues of reform before they can affect the classroom." For these reasons, we need to consider at least briefly several major forces in the socioeconomic context, namely, public finance and support, the possible teacher shortage, vast changes in knowledge and work, and the American family.

Public Finance and Support

Kirst (1986) worries that economic decline, public alienation, and growing dissatisfaction with the performance of schools might translate into diminished political support, and the shifting of federal budget priorities from education to national defense, health, and social security. "Politicians are already clamoring for results. And the reforms already in place raise numerous unanswered questions" (p. 343).

The states have substantially raised expenditures for education during the past 15 years; yet it is not clear that more funds will be easy to raise. Local school districts seem highly constrained in obtaining additional funding, even by such innovative techniques as donor funds, enterprise activities, and sharing expenses with other agencies for common activities (Odden, 1986).

A Shortage of Educators

While educational expectations and demands are rising and budgets seem threatened, the nation faces a possible shortfall of qualified educators; perhaps as many as one million new teachers will be needed in the next decade.

> Plans for higher standards, higher salaries, and higher quality people to enter teacher training programs are in a race with a growing teacher shortage. The problem is made worse by the large numbers of teachers retiring or leaving the professions for other jobs, as well as by problems of image and economics that make teaching an unattractive profession (Pipho, 1986, p. 333).

Changes in Knowledge and Work

It seems, moreover, that the "information economy" is upon us. Primary industries such as agriculture and mining are declining in their importance in the world economy. Even traditional manufacturing seems less crucial to the national well-being than high technologies and information industries.

This time of vast change is most critical for science and technology. Hurd (1986) finds that the crisis in education, particularly its scientific and techno-logical aspects, arises from the disjuncture between modern science and the existing character of science in the society and culture, between modern sci-ence and the existing character of science in the classroom.

Changes in Families

What of the first educators, parents? Children spend only about 13 percent of the waking hours of their first 18 years of life in school and 87 percent of their waking time under the nominal control of their families. Yet family pathology rates, which have profound effects on learning, have exploded in the last few decades.

During the century from 1860 to 1960, for example, the divorce rate in the United States held between 30 to 35 per thousand marriages. Fertility de-clined after 1960, non-marital cohabiting rose dramatically, and divorces in-creased to unprecedented levels. At current rates, about one-third of all American children will witness the dissolution of their parents' marriages. The percentage of working wives, moreover, rose from 32 percent in 1960 to 56 percent in 1981 (Cherlin, 1983).

The family is critical to success in school. Indeed, "the curriculum of the home" is twice as predictive of academic learning as family socioeconomic status. This curriculum involves informed parent-child conversations about everyday events, encouragement and discussion of leisure reading, monitor-ing and joint analysis of television viewing and peer activities, deferral of im-mediate gratifications to accomplish long-term goals, expressions of affection, interest in the child's academic and other progress as a person, and perhaps, among such unremitting efforts, occasional doses of caprice and serendipity. The evidence suggests that parental influence is no less important in the high school years (Walberg, 1983; Walberg and Shanahan, 1983; U.S. Department of Education, 1986).

Families, moreover, are becoming less constructively influential on char-acter. Several critical indexes of youth character—suicide, homicide, and out-of-wedlock births—showed sharp rises in the last few decades when aca-demic standards appeared to slacken, and a cafeteria of courses became in-creasingly available to high school students (Wynne and Walberg, 1984).

Given these reform demands upon schools; the possible faltering of fi-nancial and public support; a shortage of educators; changes in society, knowledge, and work; and a crisis of American families—given all these and other increasing demands and difficult conditions—educators face an im-mense challenge. Reform is needed. But who is in charge of the curriculum and its delivery? How can we decide what to do?

References

Cherlin, A. "Changing Family and Household." In *Annual Review of Sociology: Volume 9*, edited by R. H. Turner and J. F. Short. Palo Alto, Calif.: Annual Reviews, 1983.

Hurd, P. D. "Perspectives for the Reform of Science Education." *Phi Delta Kappan* 67(1986):353-358.

Kirst, M. W. "Sustaining the Momentum of State Education Reform." *Phi Delta Kappan* 67(1986):341-345.

National Association of Secondary School Principals. "Statement on National Reports." Unpublished manuscript. Reston, Va.: NASSP, 1983.

Odden, A. "Sources of Funding for Education Reform." *Phi Delta Kappan* 67(1986):335-340.

Peterson, P. E. "Did the Education Commissions Say Anything?" *Brookings Review*, Winter 1983, pp. 3-11.

Pipho, C. "Quantity vs. Quality: States Aim To Improve Teaching and Teachers." *Phi Delta Kappan* 67(1986):333-334.

Tanner, D. "The American High School at the Crossroads." *Educational Leadership* 41(1984a):4-14.

———. "Review of *Horace's Compromise.*" *Educational Leadership* 42(1984b):86-87.

U.S. Department of Education. *What Works: Research About Teaching and Learning.* Washington, D.C.: DOE, 1986.

Walberg, H. J. "Scientific Literacy and Economic Productivity in International Perspective." *Daedalus* 112(1983):1-28.

Walberg, H. J., and Shanahan, T. "High School Effects on Individual Students." *Educational Researcher* 2(1983):4-9.

Wynne, E. A., and Walberg, H. J., eds. *Developing Character: Transmitting Knowledge.* Posen, Ill.: ARL Press, 1984.

CHAPTER 4

Who Is in Charge Of the Curriculum?

Fenwick W. English

THE BASIC ASSUMPTION UNDERLYING MANY OF the national reports as well as state initiatives has been that there is a line of authority and structure in the schools that can turn them in a different direction. The belief is that with "new orders" the educational ship of state can be righted, and with a fresh start can arrive at our destination of "educational excellence."

All this effort assumes a control system that is largely mythical in the day-to-day realities of building administration in school systems. It assumes skills and knowledge that secondary principals often lack. Even if the matter of control could be easily resolved, many principals appear not to know how to:

- Use feedback data in the form of test scores to intervene in an ongoing and complex social system;
- Relate test data to curricular subject areas within or across subject matter disciplines;
- Change curricular priorities so that pupil achievement is positively affected, particularly when the curriculum has become a captive of scheduling processes in the secondary school;
- Relate curriculum to the evaluation of an isolated teacher as one part of a total effort of many people to implement an integrated educational program (English, March 1979).

What many principals do is administer pep talks and concentrate on the evaluation of the work of individual teachers in classrooms (often the worst choices).

The Dilemma of Integrating Instruction and Curriculum

Many school systems and principals have rushed to implement a new type of instructional system, such as the Madeline Hunter model, that concentrates on weak teachers to improve the overall general effectiveness within the existing school setting. But the improvement of instruction will not solve curriculum problems. If, for example, the math programs of a junior high school and a sending elementary school are not compatible, simply installing the Hunter model will not lead to improved curricular articulation. It may even make articulation worse by accentuating the differences between schools. If curriculum articulation was a problem before, it will remain a problem after the implementation of the Hunter model in such a situation.

Any instructional model's power is ensured only by the presence of a systematic curriculum upon which instruction is based. If each teacher is his or her own curriculum, no instructional model can create a curriculum that is articulated. Whatever teachers were doing, they will continue to do, perhaps better, but in isolation.

A formal curriculum is needed for any instructional model to utilize teacher and student time and interest to the maximum (English, May 1979). Curriculum is the means in a highly decentralized structure of self-contained units to tie individual actions together.

Schools can be simply collections of teachers doing their own thing, or integrated agencies aimed at accomplishing common purposes. It is to this latter goal that principals must exert their influence and know-how. Accomplishing this goal is the essence of instructional leadership.

The Shifting Locus of Control

Prior to recent large-scale initiatives (embodied in standardized testing), most principals were expected to translate district policy into local actions. This was no mean task since many school district curricular policies were extremely vague or nonexistent. Boards of education have for many years failed to develop workable and governable curricular policies within which principals and central office staff could function. Most boards do not know how to establish curricular guidelines beyond publishing a set of beliefs and setting graduation requirements by courses and subjects.

Most boards assume that the schools are working as a system although no such assumption would ever be made about financial affairs. Why boards would assume a curriculum exists without prescribing one is a mystery. Budgets don't exist unless they are required; neither do curricula. Principals must discern how their schools can function as units of a larger system. Some principals are bothered by this reality but others relish being left alone.

No one seemed to care much about resolving the matter until, with the spate of national reports, state initiatives mandated large-scale testing programs. These testing programs are intended to centralize and focus instructional efforts. Solely from an instructional viewpoint in a self-contained structure, the task seems impossible. It is only with the creation of a curriculum that it becomes manageable. A responsive curriculum pulls together, i.e., provides a focus for what teachers are expected to do in classrooms. And since the principal is the only one who looks at all classrooms simultaneously, it is to the principal that the state and the district look for the creation and maintenance of curricular cohesion.

The locus of control has shifted from a primarily local and building level one to systemwide and state focus. Tests that examine students on cumulative knowledge require a system response, not a school by school response. The high school proficiency test (HSPT) in New Jersey, for example, requiring a ninth grade student to pass in order to receive a diploma, is really an examination of the K-8 curriculum and not the secondary 9-12 curriculum. High schools can only engage in remediation. Only the elementary schools can take preventive action that will ultimately reduce the total number of student failures on the HSPT.

Tests like the New Jersey HSPT force schools to articulate their actions more closely. These tests are devices of centralization, not decentralization. They require school systems to behave as systems and not as collections or confederations of schools (English, 1985).

The considered opinion of many social scientists studying school systems reveals that they are not tightly drawn, neat line-and-staff hierarchies. School systems are "loosely coupled"; that is, they only partially work toward a group response in which the individual parts are smoothly integrated. Rather, they operate in a much more dispersed and decentralized fashion. School systems are built classroom by classroom and school by school; never simultaneously as a whole entity. School systems grow and decline by accretion of units that are generally sustained apart from one another.

Despite the fact that schools and school systems grow by accretion, they are expected, even required, to be integrated into the larger entity. Principals are supposed to know how to bring about this integration that will help the larger school system be responsive to external demands.

Schools may look like articulated entities, but only the most unusual actually are. Yet, most of the state initiatives in education assume that they are integrated. School systems have a difficult time coordinating their internal processes to be responsive to these growing external stimuli.

What Principals Face

Bringing the school into a cohesive and integrated state means knowing where the school now stands and where it must be at some point in the future. This demands conceptual knowledge of a school: what it can do, what it must do, and what it cannot do. This knowledge implies a thorough understanding of the social, technical, and work processes in schools. It means the ability to envision a school not just as separate classroom units, but as a continuous process of actions and interactions with students in a planned and cohesive way. It involves developing optimum instructional focus and capitalizing upon human energy and time, without promoting the rigidities of standardization and uniformity that can lead to an unresponsive environment.

On the other hand, the challenge of system integration rules out the romantic, naive, and uneconomical view that schools can be simple, largely unplanned, and spontaneous places where teachers do their own thing and never mind the consequences. The reality of education today makes this alternative unworkable.

What Principals Must Do

School principals who are in control of their schools know that:

- Schools are complex, highly interactive, and sensitive working environments;
- Teachers are very sensitive to job differences among themselves;
- Involvement of those affected is essential to the survival and longevity of any planned change;
- Planning is the invisible "anchor" of successful intervention; (plans not only chart things to happen, but prevent other things from happening).
- Schools are not static places, but fluid environments with people occupying various roles and engaged in a continuous process of role definition, tension, and conflict over organizational resources, and changing inter-group relationships;
- These changing relationships can be charted, monitored, and changed by purposive actions;
- A curriculum must already be established for teachers to work together in a unified and cohesive way to enhance pupil learning.

Experienced principals know that there is quite a gap between what is designated as the curriculum and what occurs in classrooms. The process of translation can make the difference between delivering a planned curriculum or sabotaging it.

The most visible aspects of the principal's job fall under the line function in most school districts. Line functions operate the school system and schools on a day-to-day basis. Staff functions support line functions. Staff functions include counseling, finance, personnel, buildings and grounds, transportation, and curriculum development. Curricular line and staff functions are illustrated in Figure 1.

Neither line nor staff functions are best served or performed in isolation from the other. The design and development of curriculum is performed by staff personnel. Good practice dictates that staff personnel involve a lot of people in curriculum development. The staff should seek counsel and advice from all levels of the line—teachers to board members. When the curriculum is ready for implementation, it is handed over to the line for delivery. Line officers (principals) implement the curriculum only after conferring with those who created and wrote it.

If the line implements the curriculum as planned, but it proves to be unworkable or unrealistic, a design problem exists. The responsibility lies with

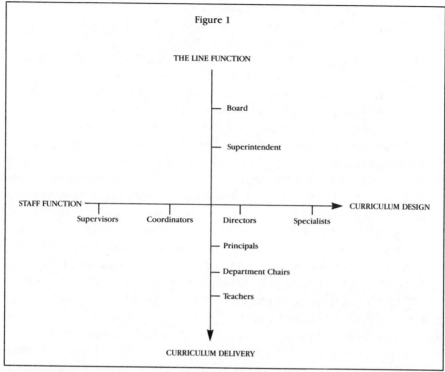

Figure 1

the staff, not the line. On the other hand, if the curriculum is appropriate, but delivered improperly, culpability is with the line, and not the staff (English and Steffy, 1983).

Principals help design curriculum, but not as their major curricular responsibility. Their major function is the management of curriculum, including staff development, monitoring, evaluation and feedback, and supervising to ensure the curriculum is properly implemented in their schools.

The principal is a curriculum generalist. (The principal may or may not possess an in-depth scholarly mastery of a particular subject discipline.) A curriculum generalist is one who understands:

- Curriculum design and the technique of curriculum alignment; i.e., ensuring congruence between the written and tested curriculum.
- Curriculum monitoring and the process of curriculum mapping. Mapping profiles time-on-task and sequence of teaching.
- Curriculum evaluation and the procedures of curriculum auditing. Auditing determines if all the elements of sound curriculum management are present.

Specifically, a curriculum generalist:

- Knows group dynamics and process skills by which any specific curriculum within any curriculum area is effectively developed;
- Is concerned about balance within and across all the disciplines of a school;

- Knows how to link the independent functions of assessment, teaching, and the written curriculum (in any form) for planned interdependence and to improve pupil performance.
- Knows how to manage the inevitable tension between line and staff, and between the various subject matter disciplines.

School reforms have almost universally assumed a subject matter or subject field view of the curriculum. Accordingly, supervisors are indispensable to the proper implementation of the curriculum. Many of the national reports make recommendations about specific additions to various subject disciplines but leave unspecified the matter of adjusting the total curriculum to accommodate these modifications. Adjustments within a discipline are the province of curricular specialists, but cross-disciplinary adjustments require someone who can see the interactions between and among the disciplines. The principal must fulfill this function for each school.

The generalist function is vital to sound curriculum management, particularly in states with statewide testing. Specialists look at a curriculum vertically (K-12); generalists look at it laterally, across subject areas.

The principal must be in charge of curriculum integration, balance, and delivery at the school level. To perform this function, the principal must know how to implement and monitor the curriculum. The difference between curriculum and instruction may be hard to distinguish in the classroom, but the principal must know how to separate them to improve student achievement. The task is never conflict-free because the learning environment is dynamic, involving people in continual interaction and decision making.

References

English, F. W. "Management Practice as a Key to Curriculum Leadership." *Educational Leadership*, March 1979, pp. 7-13.

———. "Re-Tooling Curriculum Within Ongoing School Systems." *Educational Leadership*, May 1979, pp. 7-13.

———. "Curriculum Development Within the School System." In *Considered Action for Curriculum Improvement,* edited by A. W. Foshay. Alexandria, Va.: Association for Supervision and Curriculum Development, 1980.

———. "Getting the Board Back into Curriculum Development." *MSBA Journal,* October 1984, pp. 10-13.

———. "Getting the Most from the New Jersey HSPT: A Practical Guide to Resolving Design and Delivery Problems in the Schools." Trenton, N.J.: State Department of Education, 1985.

English, F. W., and Steffy, B. "Differentiating Between Design and Delivery Problems in Achieving Quality Control in School Curriculum Management." *Educational Technology*, February 1983, pp. 29-32.

Weick, K. "Educational Organizations as Loosely Coupled Systems." *Administrative Science Quarterly*, December 1978.

CHAPTER 5

How Do You Find The Time?

James W. Keefe

A FEW YEARS AGO (1978), J. G. MARCH SAID that "educational administration is a bus schedule with footnotes by Kierkegaard." March views administration as the "rudimentary pragmatics of making organizations work—laws, rules, logistics, therapy; complicated questions of inference, the interpretation of information, and the invention and justification of actions...." School administration is a complex and demanding job. Yet most people have little or no idea what school administrators actually do. They see principals as authority figures, as community leaders, as building managers, as decisionmakers. They know the title and position; perhaps even where the principal's office is located. They see principals at community affairs and school activities. But most non-educators are unsure what a principal does on a day-to-day basis. Indeed, only part of the principal's job is visible. The invisible part usually makes the difference.

Many principals are discouraged by the kinds of demands made on them. They are buffeted by teacher groups, parental demands, central office and school board pressures, and by legislative rumbling and bumbling. Many feel they do not control their own destinies, that they have no real autonomy. Some even burn out and leave the principalship.

The principal is the single most important influence on the performance of a given school. The research confirms that principals *do* make a difference. Schools are more successful in improving student achievement when principals exercise a strong leadership role. Observers of the educational scene from James Conant to Lloyd Trump to Ernest Boyer and Theodore Sizer have stressed the pivotal role of the principal. Recent studies have linked improved student achievement and school climate directly to the daily performance of the principal. Yet principals themselves say that they spend much more time on school and personnel management than on program development (McCleary and Thomson, 1979; Keefe et al., 1983). The problem involves both time and the management of time.

Time Management

Management theorist Peter Drucker sees time analysis as a prerequisite to time management. Many managers do not analyze the way they spend their time. They allow themselves to be preoccupied by busywork. They do things themselves that should be delegated to others. They work independently of others, not collaboratively. They forget the 20/80 rule: 20 percent of one's activity produces 80 percent of the results. (Conversely, 80 percent of the activity provides only 20 percent of the results).

Finding time for instructional leadership implies establishing a system for getting things done and then sticking to it.
- Determining what the board and superintendent expect;
- Setting priorities and assessing the urgency;
- Drawing up goals and related tasks;
- Delegating as appropriate;
- Evaluating outcomes in terms of the greatest return for the time spent.

The research shows that most principals spend their time in activities that are very short, highly changeable, and often initiated by others. Peterson (1977) found that principals averaged 13 activities or contacts per hour, most limited to one or two minutes in length. Eighty-five percent of the tasks or interactions necessitated less than nine minutes of time.

Many principals do not control their time because they fail to plan its use. Indeed, many neglect to set aside quality time for program development and instructional leadership in the face of competing demands. When an angry parent drops in or a bus is delayed, many principals respond to the brush fire rather than delegate the matter and stay with their planned time use.

It does not have to be so. No matter how many crises a principal responds to, there will always be more. Crises can dominate a principal's life unless alternative plans are made and appropriate collaboration or delegation is exercised. Fire prevention is more important than fire fighting.

Crisis Management

The most important techniques for preventing school crises are early detection and clear procedures for transforming the crisis into a routine problem (Caplow, 1976). Principals can spend their time either planning for crisis management or contending separately with many crises. If principals do not define routines for crisis management, other people's crises will become their routines.

Several steps are basic to dealing with any crisis, of any magnitude. In small schools some of these steps will necessarily be truncated.
1. *Recognition of the Crisis.* The principal must learn to react early to impending crises. Whether the problem is an irate parent, a bomb scare, or a near riot, quick recognition and response is critical. Crises feed on inaction and indecision.

2. *Acceptance of Responsibility*. Crisis is no time to waste time. The principal must be, and appear to be, in charge. Even the perception by students, teachers, or the public that the principal has temporized can jeopardize the timely exercise of authority. Avoid overreacting and, at all costs, avoid an emotional reaction; but do react. In the words of the old Latin axiom: hasten slowly.

3. *Plan in Advance*. The administrative team (discussed below) can serve as a ready-made crisis council for analysis of the situation and mobilization of important personnel and resources. The secure principal realizes that he or she cannot do it alone. Preliminary plans for dealing with crises should be discussed by the team long before any incident occurs. Then crisis management can consist largely in applying the procedures already agreed upon.

4. *Implement the Plan*. Follow your planned procedures and marshal the resources at your command with the assistance of your administrative team. Delegate responsibility when your authority will not be compromised and the task is within a subordinate's competence. Good fire fighting as well as fire prevention are a team effort.

5. *Achieve Closure*. Let people know the crisis has been handled (routinely, if possible). Thank all those who assisted. Never keep any important audience in the dark. People must know that the problem has been solved and that the school is operating as usual.

The principal who prepares for crisis will have relatively few real crises to confront. And what is more important, he or she will have saved countless hours of precious time for the more important tasks of school program improvement.

Administrative Team

Collaboration is the key to effective time use and program improvement. The chief tool at the disposal of the willing principal is the administrative or supervisory-management team.

The concept of the administrative team has gained widespread credibility (but not application) in recent years. The increasing complexity of school administration and the demands made on the principal's time have prompted great interest in the concept. Most principals cannot spend the majority of their time working on instructional improvement. They need help. The administrative or supervisory-management team is a differentiated staffing approach to school management that emphasizes collaboration and complementary skills. In many schools, the principal meets regularly with an assistant principal whose responsibility is instructional improvement and perhaps scheduling, another assistant principal who supervises the student activities program, a director of student services, a building manager, and one or more departmental chairpersons. The meetings and functioning of the team are neither social nor elitist. The purpose is better school management—and better use of valuable time.

Georgiades (1984) points out that the success of the supervisory-management team depends on meeting several assumptions:

1. The responsibility for making different kinds of decisions is successfully delegated.
2. The principal and his delegates work with teachers (and students) toward instructional improvement without letting other matters interfere.
3. Allowance is made for the varying leadership styles of the participants.
4. Meetings are regularly scheduled to discuss problems and successes, and to coordinate activities.
5. Effectiveness is measured in terms of achieving the school's instructional goals.

It is important to add that successful management teams also have a formal operating protocol from the school or district board, clearly defining the decision-making model and procedures for team action.

The functioning administrative team is the first step to extending the influence of the principal and making real instructional leadership possible.

Staff Development

A principal who wants to be a successful instructional leader must involve the entire school community in the improvement process. School improvement is a collaborative process; neither administrators nor teachers can accomplish it alone. If time analysis is the key to time use and administrative collaboration the key to efficient management, then staff development is the key to involving teachers in the improvement process. Nobody supports what he does not own. Teachers must have ownership of improvement efforts for any lasting change to take place in a school.

Little (1981) has identified two norms or shared expectations that characterize staff development in particularly effective schools.

1. *Collegiality*—The expectation that teacher work is *shared* work, performed interactively with others and not solely in the isolation of the classroom.
2. *Continuous improvement*—The expectation that teacher improvement in instructional knowledge and skill is ongoing and continuous.

In highly effective schools, teachers talk with each other about teaching practices, observe one another, plan and prepare materials together, and actively teach and learn from each other. In short, successful staff development programs stimulate teachers to share and try out new instructional techniques.

Gall's (1983) work suggests that the principal is the critical resource for effective staff development. Traditional staff development assumes that teachers are and should be the primary decisionmakers about classroom instruction. But many instructional issues cannot be resolved by teachers alone. Academic requirements, homework policies, grouping practices, and even staff inservice opportunities require the involvement of administrators. Principals must set the expectations for successful staff development. In the process, they can extend their influence for appropriate program development and instructional improvement.

Collaborative staff development models generate teacher ownership and improved school climate. The Staff Development for School Improvement (SDSI) program in the metropolitan Detroit area is a case in point (Titsworth and Bonner, 1983). The six steps of the program are: 1) awareness, readiness, and commitment; 2) needs assessment; 3) planning; 4) implementation; 5) evaluation; and 6) reassessment and continuation. These same steps can be found in almost all successful change efforts. An evaluation of 19 schools after two years of the project (Sparks, 1983) showed that 82 percent of the participating teachers improved in knowledge, skills, and communication. The Detroit program operates area-wide but individual schools can achieve the same results.

Principals who support and implement systematic staff development programs are exercising one of the most important elements of instructional leadership. They are also using good organizational strategy to enhance the educational influence of their office. Trained teachers make more effective instructional leaders.

Schools Within the School

Large schools pose special problems for time management. Large schools (senior high schools with more than 1,500 students; middle level schools with more than 1,000 students) generate complexity and anonymity. Administrator's time is stretched beyond reasonable bounds. When problems multiply, the treatment of students can become quite impersonal. Management is reduced to brief contacts and standardized responses. Everyone suffers.

One very successful organizational solution to both the impersonality and the time constraints of the larger school is a school-within-a-school (SWAS) plan. The plan works particularly well with an administrative team structure in the school. SWAS organizes students and staff into smaller units, each headed by an assistant principal, subprincipal, or other administrative person. Schools can be subdivided into two, three, or four such units depending on size. Four to five hundred students has proven to be a workable number in the subschools, sometimes called units, houses, halls, or divisions.

Subschools can be organized horizontally, vertically, by programs, or any other useful grouping. Horizontal organization brings together students by grade level (9th grade unit, 10th grade unit); vertical organization includes some students of each grade level in each unit. Program organization groups students by similar programs of study (college prep, vocational, arts, humanities, gifted, etc.). Schools within the school are as self-contained as building limitations allow, to support personal contact and organizational efficiency. Weldy (1984) points out that in an "ideal" design, the subschool would contain all of the following:

- An administrator (unit principal, subprincipal)
- Guidance counselors
- Homerooms
- Some office staff
- Separate classroom facilities
- Teachers of "basic" subjects (English, math, social studies, science, and possibly foreign language).

In practice, subschools take many forms, from multiple schoolwide structures to specialized programs for the learning disadvantaged or the unmotivated. Special education programs and on-site alternative schools serve a similar purpose. The advantage of the organizational format, particularly in conjunction with an administrative team management approach, is the extension of the influence of the principal in often neglected areas of program development and instructional improvement.

Time for What?

Most people find time for what they really want to do. They also make time for what they (and others) value as most important. If program development, instructional improvement, and school effectiveness are desirable goals, principals must find time to pursue them. The administrative team, staff development, and schools within a school are only means to an end. If a principal wants to be an instructional leader, he or she will find and make the necessary time. Time is the most valuable thing we can spend. We should control the way we spend it.

References

Caplow, T. *How To Run Any Organization: A Manual of Practical Sociology*. Hinsdale, Ill.: Dryden Press, 1976.

Gall, M. D. "Using Staff Development To Improve Schools." *R&D Perspectives*, Winter 1983.

Georgiades, W. D. "Administrative Teams." In *Instructional Leadership Handbook*, edited by J.W. Keefe and J.M. Jenkins. Reston, Va.: NASSP, 1984.

Keefe, J.W.; Clark, D.C.; Nickerson, N.C., Jr.; and Valentine, J. *The Middle Level Principalship*, Volume II: The Effective Middle Level Principal. Reston, Va.: NASSP, 1983.

Little, J.W. *School Success and Staff Development*. Final report, NIE contract # 400-79-0049. Boulder, Colo.: Center for Action Research, Inc., 1981.

March, J.G. "American Public School Administration: A Short Analysis." *School Review* 86(1978):244-45.

McCleary, L.E., and Thomson, S.D. *The Senior High School Principalship*, Volume III: The Summary Report. Reston, Va.: NASSP, 1979.

Peterson, K.D. "The Principal's Task." *Administrator's Notebook* 26(1977):1-4.

Sparks, G.M. "Evaluation of the Staff Development for School Improvement Program, Final Report." Detroit, Mich.: Wayne State University, 1983.

Titsworth, G., and Bonner, C. "School Improvement in a Local Michigan School District." *Journal of Staff Development* 4(1983):120-28.

Weldy, G.R. "School-Within-a-School Organization." In *Instructional Leadership Handbook,* edited by J. W. Keefe and J.M. Jenkins. Reston, VA: NASSP, 1984.

CHAPTER 6

What About Youth At Risk?

Allan A. Glatthorn

W HAT EFFECT WILL THE RECOMMENDATIONS OF THE curriculum reform movement have on youth at risk? This is a critical question for secondary principals concerned with all students, not just the college-bound. The question can best be answered by examining briefly the curricular recommendations of the current reform movement, by assessing their likely effects on at-risk youth, and then by suggesting some alternatives to those recommendations.

The term "at-risk youth" is used throughout this article to identify those students who usually score in the lowest quartile on school achievement tests and who are in greatest danger of dropping out of school.

Curricular Recommendations

An analysis of the several commission reports and a review of several related documents indicate that current efforts to reform American schools tend to focus on three major changes that relate directly to the curriculum.

1. *Increase the number of required academic courses.* Here the specific recommendations of the National Commission (1983) are typical. According to the commission, all students seeking a high school diploma should complete the following requirements during the four years of high school: four years of English, three years of mathematics; three years of social studies; three years of science; one-half year of computer science.

2. *Increase the time for education.* Most of the reform reports recommend increasing instructional time—adding days to the school year, lengthening the school day, and making more efficient use of time.

3. *End social promotion; promote on the basis of achievement.* Several of the reform reports recommend that results on standardized achievement tests be used to determine promotion from one grade to

the next. And numerous school districts have begun to implement such achievement-based promotion policies.

In a sense, the curricular aspects of reform can be summarized in this fashion: more academics, for a longer period of time, with stricter standards.

The Probable Impact on Youth at Risk

While it is relatively simple to express strong opinions about the likely impact of such changes, it is much more difficult to make an objective assessment. All we can do is examine the available evidence and draw some tentative inferences.

The Impact: More Academics

In assessing the impact of increasing academic requirements, it would be useful to differentiate between likely effects on college preparatory students and at-risk youth. In general the research suggests that college preparatory students would benefit from such an emphasis. A careful review of the evidence by Alexander and Pallas (1983) concluded that the test scores of students who completed the "new basics" are considerably higher than the scores of those who do not. Such a conclusion seems reasonable enough: more courses in mathematics should improve scores on mathematics tests.

But even for college preparatory youth, the findings are not conclusive. Here a study by Echternacht (1977) is illuminating. He compared high schools in which SAT scores had remained stable or increased slightly between 1965 and 1976 with a group whose scores had declined more than the national average. The differences in the number of academic courses in the two groups of schools were insignificant. The English curricula were highly similar. Pass-fail grading and non-traditional offerings had expanded to the same extent. Many high schools with decreasing scores had increased the amount of homework and basic skills instruction.

What would be the effects on at-risk youth? A review of the evidence leads to the conclusion that the effects would in general be more negative than positive. Since this is one of the central concerns of this chapter, let me analyze this issue at somewhat greater length.

The new basics would result in an inequitable allocation of resources. While there are some who argue that no essential conflict exists between excellence and equity, I believe that there is a pervasive tension between our interest in achieving excellence and our concern for equity. Resources are finite—and shrinking. Every dollar allocated to funding the new basics is a dollar taken from programs for the less able.

For at-risk youth, more mathematics is not better mathematics. One of the pervasive weaknesses of all the reform pronouncements is that they have almost totally ignored the issue of curricular quality, an issue that is especially relevant for at-risk youth who seem to have less tolerance for boredom and banality. Observe the salient attributes of low-track classes that Goodlad (1984) noted in his comparisons of high and low-track sections: more rote learning; more emphasis on conforming as opposed to independent thinking; lower student satisfaction; less teacher clarity, enthusiasm, and organization; and, from the students' perceptions, more punitive and less caring teachers. We don't need more of that kind of learning.

Increasing the academic requirements is likely to lead to increased failure for at-risk youth. It is quite probable that additional courses in social studies, science, and mathematics will use the same approaches as those now used, approaches that by their nature seem not very effective for at-risk youth. Wehlage (1983) observes that the "best kind" of academic course in the traditional high school program frequently presupposes the ability of students to engage in abstract thinking. For the marginal student who has not made the transition to this type of thinking, instruction seems to be carried on in a foreign language. If past practice is any criterion, it seems unlikely that at-risk youth will receive the kind of instruction they need to make the transition to abstract thinking.

Focusing on the high school curriculum ignores the fact that for at-risk youth the earlier years are more critical. There is a growing body of evidence that the elementary grades are the crucial years for at-risk youth. Here Becker and Gersten's (1982) research is instructive. Their review of follow-up studies of intervention programs concludes that children in Follow Through programs who have made great gains in primary reading and mathematics are likely to lose ground against their middle-income peers if they do not receive high quality instruction in the intermediate grades. And Alexander and Cook (1982) note that experiences during the primary grades may be of greatest consequences for later achievement.

Thus, a reasoned analysis of the available evidence suggests that increasing academic requirements will serve in general to penalize at-risk youth.

The Impact: More Time

The argument that providing increased time will result in greater achievement has both a common-sense appeal and some support in the literature. It seems reasonable to conclude that providing more time to learn will result in greater learning, and there is a body of evidence to support that conclusion. However, there also is some evidence to the contrary. First, Husén (1967) observes in his IEA study of international mathematics achievement that the amount of instructional time and the amount of homework time had only small effects on achievement. And Stedman and Smith's 1983 review of all the comparative data on achievement across nations leads them to conclude that cultural factors are more important than time allotments.

Further doubt about the efficacy of simply increasing time is shed by an interesting study by Levin, Glass, and Meister (1984) who analyzed the cost-effectiveness of four interventions for improving reading and mathematics scores: cross-age tutoring, computer-assisted instruction, reduced class size, and increased instructional time. Their analysis led them to conclude that cross-age tutoring would be highest in cost-effectiveness, and increased instructional time would yield the least benefit in relation to cost.

So we may reasonably conclude that increasing the time devoted to academic subjects will have a modest effect, if any, on the achievement of at-risk youth. There are some clear negative effects that might result from increasing the total amount of school time (McDill, Natriello, and Pallas, 1985). These authors note that increasing the amount of time students spend in school will reduce the amount of time that at-risk students can work outside of school. They cite evidence that indicates that moderate levels of work involvement may have beneficial effects on young adolescents. They also point out that increasing the amount of school time will obviously limit the time that at-risk youth can give to extracurricular activities, with dire consequences. "Cutbacks in extracurricular activities due to increased school time may deprive the school of the only holding power it has for those high-risk students" (p. 426).

The Impact: Rigorous Promotional Standards

The final proposition is that students should be promoted solely on the basis of achievement, rather than on the basis of chronological age. There is a relatively simple standard to assess the likely impact of this proposed change on at-risk youth. In a quite objective review of 44 carefully designed studies, Holmes and Matthews (1984) conclude that the retention of elementary and junior high pupils has the following negative effects:

1. Their achievement in the subsequent year is lower.
2. They make a less satisfactory emotional adjustment.
3. They have a diminished self-image.
4. They have a less positive attitude toward school.

It thus seems reasonable to conclude that all those at-risk youth who are retained in junior high school will simply waste one year—growing older.

More Effective Alternatives

Several options are already at hand that would seem to have greater power for improving the educational lives of at-risk youth.

Quality in Curriculum

I argue for a sharply focused curriculum that sacrifices breadth for depth, coverage for understanding, and quantity for quality. My review of curricula developed especially for at-risk youth indicates that most attempt to cover too much content, dwell on inconsequential learnings, and result in mind-numbing repetition of content.

What would characterize an effective curriculum for at-risk youth? The following features seem worthy of note.

- An emphasis on critical thinking and problem solving. While much current interest exists in teaching critical thinking in schools, most of these new and revised courses seem designed for more able youth. We need instead to take special pains to improve the thinking and problem-solving skills of at-risk youth.
- An emphasis on developing concepts and improving vocabulary. Most curricula for at-risk students are so concerned with the understanding of information and the application of rote learning that concept development is slighted. If we sharply reduce the information load of the curriculum, then teachers can spend more time teaching the key concepts in each discipline. Such an emphasis on concepts and vocabulary would improve both understanding in that discipline and reading comprehension. After reviewing the research on the teaching of reading and language to the disadvantaged, Becker (1977) concludes that teaching vocabulary concept knowledge would be the single most effective way of improving reading comprehension.
- An appropriate use of the life experiences of at-risk youth. Curricular relevance may not be a popular topic today, but the testimony of successful teachers strongly suggests that there are effective ways to use the life experiences of at-risk youth without trivializing the curriculum or invading their privacy.

An Improved Instructional Technology

The second major change needed is the implementation of an improved instructional technology for at-risk youth—an important change by and large ignored by the reformers. Let me merely sketch in the key features of such a technology, since much of the research has been widely disseminated and discussed.

1. For part of their instruction, teachers of at-risk youth would use the basic instructional processes that have proved to be effective with such students. Brophy's (1982) summary is useful here:

- Approach instruction with a positive attitude that such students can learn.
- Use time efficiently so that ample opportunity to learn is provided.
- Manage the classroom efficiently and plan instruction carefully.
- Pace students rapidly, in small steps, with a high success rate.
- Use active teaching strategies, with much demonstrating, explaining, and active engagement.
- Teach to mastery by making sure that new knowledge and skills are mastered to the point of overlearning.
- Provide a supportive learning environment.

2. For part of their instruction, teachers would make effective use of co-operative learning strategies supplemented by appropriate individualization. One of the most promising instructional strategies for use with at-risk youth seems to be Team Assisted Individualization (TAI), which Slavin (1980) notes is a cooperative learning intervention specifically developed to improve the outcomes of mainstreaming for mildly academically handicapped youth. TAI uses a combination of cooperative learning and individualization that has been demonstrated effective in improving attitudes, behavior, and achievement with these learners.

3. For part of their instruction, teachers in academic classes would make appropriate use of computers to teach information-processing skills and essential concepts, and to provide diagnosis and remediation. Rather than suggesting that every student take one semester of computer science, as the National Commission recommends, it makes more sense to use computers extensively throughout the curriculum for at-risk youth. These students do not need a basic course in computer literacy; they need to use the computer as an important learning tool. The widespread use of computers in the home may widen the gap between poor and middle-class children unless the schools make computers widely available to all at-risk youth.

We have the pieces of this instructional technology already available; we need only the will, the resources, and the know-how to put the system into place.

Experiential Learning Through Field Experiences

One of the most promising means of improving the achievement and facilitating the development of at-risk youth is the use of field experiences to provide experiential learning. Wehlage (1983) makes a very cogent argument for this intervention. He points out that the most critical need of marginal high school students is what he terms "social bonding," a developmental process for achieving attachment, commitment, belief, and involvement in the life of home and school. Two things are required for such social bonding to develop: the adolescent must develop the ability to use abstract thinking; and the adolescent must shift from an egocentric to a sociocentric point of view. Wehlage faults the usual remedies applied to marginal youth—remediation, vocational skills training, and job experience—for not facilitating either of these essential types of growth. His review of the evidence indicates that experiential education, through carefully directed field experiences, has the potential to facilitate the broad development of marginal youth.

An earlier version of this article was presented at a conference sponsored by Research for Better Schools in Philadelphia, May, 1985.

References

Alexander, K. L., and Cook, M. S. "Curricula and Coursework: A Surprising Ending to a Familiar Story." *American Sociological Review* 47(1982):626-40.

Alexander, K. L., and Pallas, A. M. "Curriculum Reform and School Performance: An Evaluation of the 'New Basics.' " Baltimore, Md.: Johns Hopkins University, Center for the Social Organization of Schools, 1983.

Becker, W. C. "Teaching Reading and Language to the Disadvantaged—What We Have Learned from Field Research." *Harvard Educational Review* 47(1977):518-43.

Becker, W. C., and Gersten, R. "A Follow-Up of Follow Through: The Later Effects of the Direct Instruction Model on Children in Fifth and Sixth Grades." *American Educational Research Journal* 19(1982):75-92.

Brophy, J. "Successful Teaching Strategies for the Inner City Child." *Phi Delta Kappan* 63(1982):527-30.

Echternacht, G. J. "A Comparative Study of Secondary Schools with Different Score Patterns." (Appendix to College Board, *On Further Examination.*) New York: College Board, 1977.

Goodlad, J. I. *A Place Called School: Prospects for the Future.* New York: McGraw-Hill, 1984.

Holmes, C. T., and Matthews, K. M. "The Effects of Nonpromotion on Elementary and Junior High School Pupils: A Meta-Analysis." *Review of Educational Research* 54(1984):225-36.

Husén, T., ed. *International Study of Achievement in Mathematics: A Comparison Between Twelve Countries,* Vol. 2. New York: Wiley, 1967.

Levin, H. M.; Glass, G. V.; and Meister, G. R. *Cost Effectiveness of Four Educational Interventions.* Stanford, Calif.: Stanford University, Institute for Research on Educational Finance and Governance, 1984.

McDill, E. L.; Natriello, G.; and Pallas, A. M. "Raising Standards and Retaining Students: The Impact of the Reform Recommendations on Potential Dropouts." *Review of Educational Research* 55(1985):415-33.

National Commission on Excellence in Education. *A Nation at Risk: The Imperative for School Reform.* Washington, D.C.: Government Printing Office, 1983.

Slavin, R. E. "Cooperative Learning." *Review of Educational Research* 50(1980):315-42.

Stedman, L. C., and Smith, M. S. "Recent Reform Proposals for American Education." *Contemporary Education Review* 2(1983):85-104.

Wehlage, G. G. "The Marginal High School Student: Defining the Problem and Searching for Policy." *Children and Youth Services Review* 5(1983):321-42.

CHAPTER 7

Should We Cut The Curriculum?

Fenwick W. English

A FLOOD OF NATIONAL REFORMS HAS CASCADED into 50 state capitals and resulted in a variety of new initiatives to upgrade and improve secondary school curricula (*Education Week*, 1985). These thrusts have met with little opposition since they are heralded as means of re-establishing rigor or creating new standards of excellence.

Many of the reforms challenge the underlying assumption of the comprehensive high school (Trump and Baynham, 1961), which has been dominant so long in American public education. That ideal holds that the public high school should be a diverse place, offering something for everyone. A single-track curriculum was inappropriate for such a secondary school since it had to serve many diverse constituencies.

While that notion has not been directly broached, increased state requirements for math, science, and foreign language have crowded out many of the electives designed to serve a variety of student interests at the secondary school. These courses held students in school because they met their individual requirements and interests.

What many legislators have failed to understand is that if available time is not expanded with added requirements, new mandates force out student options within the unchanged school day. There is a kind of pernicious "law of displacement" that squeezes out some parts of the curriculum and keeps others. One result is an (already) escalating dropout rate (*Baltimore News American*, 1985).

Confronted with the problems of limited time, expanded requirements, and disappearing electives, the secondary school principal more than ever must be knowledgeable about:

- The nature of the student body, its outlook on life, and environmental and community influences;
- Student prior educational achievement levels and expectations;
- The characteristics and capabilities of the faculty;
- The nature and quality of program support services;

● The type of facilities and equipment/technology available for instruction.

How the principal leads the school will depend on which of three major curriculum viewpoints is predominant in state level initiatives and how the principal blends them together at the operational level. These three viewpoints are the:

1. nature of knowledge
2. nature of society
3. nature of learning.

If the principal is disposed toward the "nature of knowledge" focus (Tyler, 1949), then he or she will be most concerned with the constitution or variability of the "core curriculum." Far less emphasis will be placed on vocational concerns or psychological theory as points of reference for curriculum shaping. This view of the curriculum is most often espoused by educational critics like Mortimer Adler (1982). From this perspective a balanced curriculum is one in which emphasis is on the "classics." For Adlerians, cutting electives and vocational offerings is a move toward re-establishing "balance."

The "nature of society" focus for curriculum development has long been dominant in the curriculum field. Called by some the social-utilitarian approach (English, 1986), this approach to curriculum development uses societal survival skills as the point of departure for determining curriculum balance. The idea is as old as Franklin Bobbitt's original work on curriculum (1918).

The social-utilitarians see curriculum as a means to an end and not an end in itself. The curriculum is a deliberately shaped instrument to attain the desired and required social skills and knowledge. At the core of the approach lies the concept of needs assessment (English and Kaufman, 1975). From needs analysis, a curriculum is created to produce the outcomes deemed necessary from the schooling process. The social-utilitarian model has been the dominant idea behind much of the "accountability movement" of the past two decades (Wise, 1979).

The social-utilitarians see knowledge not so much as static and inflexible, but shifting and embedded in a sea of cultural values that change over time and vary across cultures. There are few constants so no one curriculum or course would be good for everybody or for all time.

This view is decidedly at odds with the view that the curriculum is something for all time and impregnable to societal fads and trends at any particular time. This basic clash of views about curriculum and what it comprises has been going on for decades. It is not likely to be resolved in the foreseeable future. Principals should view this conflict as the continuous process of sifting the knowledge base for what is most important.

The third focus of curriculum is the nature of learning. Educators who lean more heavily in this direction start with ideas about human learning as the initial step in shaping curriculum. They are influenced by scholars like

Bruner, Piaget, and Kohlberg. Curriculum should "fit" the way humans learn and not the other way around. Knowledge does not exist apart from the learner.

Some contemporary educational thinkers insist that society is not "out there" waiting to be discovered by the learner, but rather society is constantly taking on a structure as perceived by the learner. This dynamic interaction between the learner and society negates the idea that curriculum exists apart from the learner (Rabil, 1967).

Curriculum Decisions and Balance

If a district or school approaches the question of curriculum balance believing that the nature of knowledge should dominate the discussion, the course catalog will reflect a highly traditional curriculum packed with math and science and the classics. There will be few electives. The curriculum will look much like that in many of the nation's established private schools. It will be almost exclusively college oriented.

If the district or school is swayed by the idea that students must have a salable skill, be competent citizens, participate in a swiftly changing technological world, the curriculum will contain major options. The options will focus on social survival, and vocational and collegiate preparation. Balance in this kind of curriculum attempts to confront the needs of different students.

If the district/school concentrates on the nature of the learner and learning, then balance assumes a wholly different perspective. In this context, balance is a matter of reflecting human growth and selecting those curricular options that stimulate and encourage human growth. The actual content of the curriculum is much less important than its impact on the learner.

One of the contradictions in the current educational debate is that the social-utilitarian argument is used as the basis for declaring the curriculum inadequate (in such national statements as *The Nation at Risk*), but the antidote in no way represents a pragmatic mix of courses to cope with the changing world scene. Conservatives, for example, generally offer only the classical curriculum as the "correct solution."

Because society is rapidly moving toward a new foundation in technology and information processing (Naisbitt, 1982), the curriculum will have to stay somewhat fluid. If the curriculum is allowed to become fixed at any particular stage of this movement, curricular obsolescence will be a real problem for secondary schools.

The decisions a principal must make concerning curricular balance are these:

1. What is the data base for examining the curriculum?
2. How reliable and valid is that base, how prone to obsolescence?
3. Given the nature of the data and the identifiable societal trends, what should the curricular constants be?

4. How much room exists for curricular options?
5. How many variations are possible within any configuration of curricular constants to options?
6. What kinds of evaluation data are necessary to determine if a given configuration of curricular constants/options is defensible? Should we engage in curricular change?

Perhaps the last question is most important. What kind of information will cause the secondary school to re-examine its curricular configuration? Many schools today do not know the answer to that question, much less have any idea (without external mandates) when to seriously ponder meaningful curriculum change.

Rare indeed today is a secondary school striving for curricular balance that is not subject to competing external/internal pressures to cut costs, reduce frills, raise standards, teach the basics, promote a love of learning, and reduce dropouts. All of these objectives are treated by the media as slogans, and by the media and some of the public as synonyms. The principal is expected to restore or establish a wholeness to these competing objectives.

Yet raising standards and reducing frills are by no means synonymous. Nor does teaching the basics automatically result in excellence. A balanced curriculum depends largely on how one defines curriculum and balance. Indeed, the fact that not everyone means the same thing by the same words is part of the problem.

A Model for Integration

One possible model for integration of the secondary school curriculum that includes all three conceptual approaches was proposed by Cawelti (1974). The model reorganizes the high school curriculum into five basic clusters: (1) learning skills, (2) health, physical education, and leisure, (3) career education, (4) cultural studies, and (5) societal skills.

Figure 1 illustrates how these five clusters would be integrated into three aspects of school life: (1) academics, (2) aesthetics, and (3) athletics. The model erases the common distinctions between the curriculum and the cocurriculum and adopts the point of view that there is only one curriculum that is totally integrative in the experience of the student.

Indeed, the existing American curriculum resulted from the need to find outlets for youthful energy, to give a place to popular sports activities, and to reach into communities for appropriate curricular extensions. Cocurricular activities have experienced some problems, but have a solid place in the life of the typical secondary school. Finding the correct balance or interdependence among competing realms has been particularly difficult for the social-utilitarians because of their concern for the currency of the curriculum. Some of the current reforms have led to stringent new rules on athletic participation for some students (most famous is the Texas "no pass, no play"

Figure 1
A Model for the Integration of the High School Curriculum

CAWELTI'S CURRICULUM CLUSTERS	ACADEMICS	AESTHETICS	ATHLETICS
LEARNING SKILLS	MATH READING LISTENING WRITING PROBLEM SOLVING	TECHNIQUES TO PERFORM	SKILLS REQUIRED TO PLAY, COMPETE
HEALTH, PE, AND LEISURE	SCIENCE/HEALTH HAZARDS	APPRECIATION ALTERNATIVE LIFESTYLES	PHYSICAL DEVELOPMENT LIFETIME SPORTS
CAREER EDUCATION	WORK ETHICS DIGNITY OF WORK	AESTHETICS OF WORK	DISCIPLINE POISE SELF-CONFIDENCE LEADERSHIP
CULTURAL STUDIES	ETHNIC STUDIES HUMANITIES	ART MUSIC THEATER ARCHITECTURE	VIEWS OF GAMES PLAY COMPETITION
SOCIETAL SKILLS	CIVICS HISTORY ECONOMICS	FASHIONS LIFESTYLES LEISURE ACTIVITIES	PHYSICAL FITNESS INTERPERSONAL SKILLS LEADERSHIP/ DEPENDENCY FRIENDSHIPS

NOTES: (1) The curriculum clusters were extrapolated from G. Cawelti, *Vitalizing the High School* (ASCD, 1974)

(2) The model is used with permission from Educational Research Service. It appeared in F. English, "Balance in the School Curriculum: Today's Directions and Dilemmas," (ERS, *Spectrum,* Winter 1986).

law), but most states have tempered their response and avoided extreme positions.

The school's socialization role in the larger society has been conspicuously overlooked in the recent national reports. The socialization process is most heavily embedded in the cocurriculum, a fact that must be kept firmly in mind by any school entertaining thoughts of preventing large numbers of students from participating. If the nation's secondary schools are to be more than places to train the elite, achieving an integrative view of the curriculum and the cocurriculum is more compelling than ever.

References

Adler, M. *The Paideia Proposal: An Educational Manifesto*. New York: Macmillan Co., 1982.

Bobbitt, F. *The Curriculum*. Boston: Houghton Miflin, 1918.

Bruner, J. S. *Toward a Theory of Instruction*. Cambridge, Mass.: Harvard University Press, 1966.

Cawelti, G. *Vitalizing the High School*. Washington, D.C.: Association for Supervision and Curriculum Development, 1974.

"Changing Course: A 50 State Summary of Reform Measures." *Education Week*, February 6, 1985, pp. 1-30.

English, F. "Balance in the School Curriculum: Today's Directions and Dilemmas." *Spectrum,* Winter 1986, pp. 9-15.

English, F., and Kaufman, R. "Needs Assessment: A Focus for Curriculum Development." Washington, D.C.: Association for Supervision and Curriculum Development, 1975.

"Keeping Poor Students Poor." *Baltimore News American,* February 4 1985.

Kohlberg, L. "Development of Moral Character and Ideology." In *Review of Child Development Research*, edited by M. L. Hoffman. New York: Macmillan Co., 1979.

Naisbitt, J. *Megatrends*. New York: Warner Books, 1982.

Rabil, A. *Merleau-Ponty: Existentialist of the Social World*. New York: Columbia University Press, 1967.

Trump, J. L., and Baynham, D. *Guide to Better Schools*. Chicago, Ill.: Rand McNally, 1961.

Tyler, R. *Curriculum Syllabus*. Chicago, Ill.: University of Chicago Press, 1949.

Wise, A. E. *Legislated Learning*. Berkeley, Calif.: University of California, 1979.

CHAPTER 8

How Does the School Schedule Affect The Curriculum?

Allan A. Glatthorn

TOO MANY EXPERTS WHO HAVE BEEN bent on reforming the secondary school curriculum seem to have been insensitive to the important role the school schedule plays in both constraining and facilitating such efforts. The schedule and the curriculum are closely linked. In a sense, the school schedule can be seen as a package for delivering the curriculum. The size and shape of this package have an impact on the contents. Effective principals are sensitive to this relationship. They take steps to ensure that their school schedule is the most appropriate one for their curricular goals. Following are some specific steps that principals can take to build a better scheduling package for their curriculum.

Time and the Curriculum

The schedule is the chief means for allocating time in schools. The following three steps will help to ensure that this critical resource is used effectively.

1. Check time allocations so that they reflect curricular priorities. How many hours of instruction should be provided during the school year for science and how many for art? That question focuses on the critical issue of time allocations across different subjects. (Time allocations within a particular subject are discussed below.) To a certain extent, of course, the question is answered by state requirements and district policies, especially at the high school level.

If some flexibility exists, however, principals must be sure that the decisions to increase or decrease the time allotted to a given subject reflect current priorities. The research supports the common-sense notion that, in general, the more time allocated to a particular subject, the better is student achievement in that subject (Denham and Lieberman, 1980).

In reflecting on this key issue of time allocations and curricular priorities, resist the temptation to jump on the "more" bandwagon. Almost all the major reform efforts have reached the simplistic conclusion that requiring more mathematics, more science, and more foreign language will solve our educational problems. While the research in general supports the conclusion that increasing academic requirements can result in better achievement scores, the use of that additional time is more important than its mere provision.

No one questions the importance of academic achievement, but improved education is more than high scores on College Board examinations. Here it is appropriate to summarize the conclusions of the ASCD Task Force on Increased High School Graduation Requirements (1985).

- The most academically able students appear to be least affected by increased graduation requirements.
- Negative consequences are more likely for high school students who do not go on to college.
- Inadequate attention has been paid to the need for a carefully balanced program of general education that includes requirements in the arts and humanities.

And, as Chapter 6 of this work indicates, educational leaders intent on planning the best programs for at-risk youth will have to do more than add one additional year of science and mathematics.

2. Defend instructional time.   Once time has been allocated, guard against unnecessary and excessive intrusions. There is a body of research which suggests that in effective schools, the principal defends instructional time by adopting and enforcing a firm policy on early dismissals and classroom interruptions (Purkey and Smith, 1983). Doing so is difficult; the secondary principal is always subject to strong pressures from several directions to excuse students, to dismiss classes, and to make public-address announcements. A wise principal knows how to protect instructional time without making the school an academic pressure-cooker.

One approach is to use a rotating period schedule. Since the last period of the school day is the one most often subject to interruptions, some secondary schools have found it helpful to use a schedule rotation that allows a class to meet the last period on Monday, the first period on Tuesday, and the third on Wednesday. All classes rotate through the troublesome final time slot to soften the impact on any single one.

3. Help teachers allocate time appropriately within a subject.   Suppose that a school allocates 140 hours to English in the hope of improving student writing, but most English teachers devote only 25 hours of the total to the teaching of writing. Not much progress will be made toward the goal of improved writing. Be sure that the time allocated within a subject reflects the relative importance of the various components of that subject. And teachers must be active participants in this discussion for any change to occur.

How do you accomplish the goal of balance within a subject?

- Written curriculum guides should indicate the relative importance of curricular components and suggest some general time allocations. If present guides do not include such information, set up committees within each subject area to develop tentative guidelines and then establish a process for faculty and district review.

- Teachers should receive help from subject-matter specialists in making yearly, semester, and unit plans that reflect agreed-upon priorities. The research suggests that this help is most productive at the beginning of the school year (Clark and Yinger, 1980). In the first few weeks, teachers make planning decisions that affect the rest of the year.

- Develop with the teachers a curriculum monitoring plan that provides reliable data on how much time teachers actually allocate to curricular components. Teacher involvement in developing the plan is essential, since many teachers believe that curriculum monitoring diminishes their professional role and represents administrative distrust. A quarterly written report from the teacher to the department head or team leader is one acceptable method.

- Supervisory conferences, whenever appropriate, should include questions of time allocation within the subject: "How much time have you allocated to this unit? How do you make decisions about time allocations?"

The Schedule and Teacher Curriculum

There is a written curriculum—what curriculum guides suggest should be emphasized; and a taught curriculum—what teachers actually teach. The research suggests that the two are not very similar. Most secondary teachers pay only scant attention to written guides as they develop their own curriculum (Cusick, 1983). In a sense, then, the teacher is the ultimate curriculum specialist in your school or district.

The research also suggests that the typical teacher is not a very successful curriculum maker. Some recent studies indicate that teachers are so concerned with classroom management that their curricula concentrate on making classroom life easier to manage (Doyle, 1986). For example, teachers may reduce complex written curricula for teaching higher order thinking skills to simplified exercises that focus on comprehension and memory. This curricular simplification helps them to reduce planning and to use familiar instructional methods, thus enabling them to devote more time and energy to classroom management.

In dealing with this problem, it is probably unwise to prohibit teachers from modifying and adapting district-developed curricula. The attempts during the 1960s to develop "teacher-proof curricula" failed almost totally. Teachers are jealous of their roles as curriculum makers, and once behind the classroom door, have almost complete autonomy.

What can be done to improve teachers' curriculum-making skills? Staff development is part of the answer. Two types of scheduling decisions can also play a part.

1. Provide time in the school schedule for team planning.   Virtually all secondary teachers get a preparation period, which often turns out to be a time to relax. These breaks from the burden of teaching are essential; teaching is a demanding responsibility. In addition to such breaks, however, teaching teams must be able to meet during the school day on a regular basis for instructional planning and curriculum modification.

Principals must exercise leadership to help instructional teams use such time effectively. The master schedule can permit teaching teams to be free at the same time, preferably for two consecutive periods. In addition, department heads or team leaders will need special training in curriculum modification and group problem solving. Principals should work with team leaders in developing some reasonable system of accountability. If time is provided for curricular work, what results are expected?

2. Reduce the number of teacher preparations.   A teacher who has only one or two types of classes to prepare for will probably do a better job of planning than a teacher who has four or five different preparations. It seems reasonable that reducing the number of preparations will enhance the quality of curriculum making. Obviously, this step will be difficult in smaller schools where staff resources are spread thin. Any degree of reduction will be helpful.

Grouping and the Curriculum

One of the most critical variables in the school schedule is the way in which students are grouped for instruction. Grouping practices have often been attacked by critics as one of the most pernicious elements of the hidden curriculum. The following indictment is typical:

> The pedagogical foundation for democratic processes in the classroom can be established by eliminating the pernicious practice of "tracking" students. This tradition in schools of grouping students according to "abilities" and perceived performance is of dubious instructional value (Giroux and Penna, 1979).

There are two problems with such an indictment. The first is that the authors ignore a rather important distinction between ability grouping—sorting students into ability-based groups for instruction (such as high, average, and low ability)—and curriculum grouping—sorting students into such curricular tracks as vocational, general, and college preparatory. The second serious problem is that the empirical evidence available does not unqualifiedly support their assertions, at least with respect to ability grouping.

Because the distinction between ability and curriculum grouping is so important, it makes sense to examine both kinds of grouping in relation to the schedule and the curriculum.

What is the evidence on ability grouping? A meta-analysis by Kulik and Kulik (1982) of 52 secondary school studies of ability and heterogeneous grouping highlighted these findings.

1. In more than 70 percent of the studies, students from grouped classes outperformed ungrouped students by a small amount. The effects were largest in special classes for the gifted and talented.

2. Ability grouping seemed to have a positive effect on student attitudes toward the subject taught.

3. Students who were grouped by ability tended to have a better attitude toward school and a higher self-concept, although these effects were smaller and less consistent.

In addition, a major study (Sanford, 1980) of more than 100 junior high classes concluded that increased heterogeneity of classes was associated with these drawbacks: teachers were less able to respond to individual learning needs; teachers were less able to respond to students' affective needs; there was less task engagement; and achievement gains of lower ability students tended to be lower.

On the other hand, Slavin's (1986) "best-evidence synthesis" of more than 50 elementary school studies on various forms of ability grouping "refutes the assertion that ability grouped class assignment can increase student achievement in elementary schools." Slavin separately reviewed ability grouped class assignment, regrouping for reading and mathematics, ability grouping for reading across grades (Joplin Plan); non-graded plans and within-class ability grouping. Slavin's findings included the following:

1. Assigning students to self-contained classes by general achievement or ability does not enhance student achievement.

2. Some cross-grade ability grouping plans in selected subjects can increase achievement, specifically the Joplin Plan and use of multiple grouping for different subjects in non-graded programs.

3. Within-class ability grouping in mathematics is effective.

4. Ability grouping is most effective for one or two subjects with students in heterogeneous classes most of the day, when group assignment really reduces heterogeneity in a specific skill and group assignments are frequently reassessed, and when teachers vary the level and pace of instruction according to student needs.

Of course, the evidence is not conclusive. Many educators believe that heterogeneity has special advantages that must be considered. Heterogeneous classes are more likely to reflect the ethnic mix of the student body, and it is desirable for students of differing abilities to learn from and with each other, especially in subjects like social studies and English, where diversity of viewpoint is important.

Since the issues are so complex and teachers seem to feel so deeply about them, it makes good sense to involve the entire faculty in examining whether present grouping practices seem to be meeting the school's educational goals and in making whatever modifications seem necessary. Once grouping decisions have been made, principals should work with teachers in evaluating the curricula for the different groups, paying special attention to the curriculum for the less able.

The practice of curriculum grouping or tracking, in which students follow a predetermined career-oriented program, such as college preparatory or vocational, is more clear-cut. Rosenbaum's (1980) review of the research is most enlightening. He notes that there is no clear finding from the research on whether ability or social class is the primary determiner of track placement. According to several studies, the guidance counselor plays a key role in track selections. Many students, according to Rosenbaum, are in curricular tracks that are inconsistent with their career choices. The lack of congruence is complicated by the fact that although curricular tracking is relatively stable, more movement takes place from college preparatory to general and vocational than the other way around.

The chief problem with curriculum tracking, according to researchers, is the lack of challenge in the curriculum for general or non-college preparatory students. Several studies concluded that college preparatory classes have better content, pedagogy, and class climate than non-college preparatory. And teachers in general track classes conveyed lower expectations and spent more time enforcing the rules.

Many experts therefore believe that rigid curriculum tracking should be eliminated, except for those students electing to attend a separate vocational-technical school. All other students can probably profit more from an untracked program, assisted by guidance counselors and teachers in making course choices that give them several post-high school options.

The Schedule and Curriculum Content: Big Ideas in Little Boxes

The final problem involving the schedule and the curriculum is perhaps the most complex and the most difficult to solve. The typical secondary schedule of five 45-minute classes per week is probably the most ineffective way to teach students. Any learning activity that involves discovering, problem solving, and creating needs longer blocks of time. A foreign language is probably best learned by "total immersion" in which students spend the whole day studying and speaking the language. And school-sponsored community service and external mentorships obviously require extended periods of time.

The 5 × 45 schedule persists for some good reasons. Student attention seems to flag in longer periods. Many teachers find it difficult to handle extended time blocks and prefer the more frequent breaks of the traditional schedule. And old habits and practices are just very difficult to change. But, the 5 × 45 schedule continues to act as a serious constraint on curricular innovation. All learning (except where extended laboratory classes are provided) must be packaged into discrete 35-minute instructional segments.

Periodically over the years, systematic attempts have been made to break away from the 5 × 45 schedule. In the 1960s, many secondary schools, responding to the innovative ideas of J. Lloyd Trump, experimented with modular schedules in which the schedule was built around 20-minute time modules. In this type of schedule, an English class might be 20 minutes on Monday, 40 minutes on Wednesday, and 60 minutes on Thursday and Friday. Most schools have since abandoned the modular schedule and have returned to traditional patterns. Many teachers had great difficulty in adapting to and using both the shorter and longer periods of time. Some administrators experienced problems in building and managing the modular schedule.

The "block of time" schedule seems to have more staying value, at least in middle schools. In the block-of-time schedule, a multi-disciplinary team of teachers is given an extended period of time (such as 135 minutes) to teach a large group of students; the teachers decide, usually week by week, how they will use that time. Some research indicates that effective middle schools have evolved block-of-time schedules that are used in special ways to meet the needs of their students (Lipsitz, 1984).

High school principals who feel their faculties are not ready for such extensive innovation may wish to begin by encouraging teachers of English, social studies, mathematics, and foreign language to use an extended "laboratory" period once a week to provide learning activities of greater depth and substance. One obvious caution holds here. If teachers opt for a laboratory period in the academic subjects, they will have to modify the curriculum to include learning objectives and activities that can be pursued profitably in the extended period. If teachers do not change the curriculum, not much will be gained in modifying the standard schedule.

References

ASCD Task Force on Increased Graduation Requirements. *With Consequences for All.* Alexandria, Va.: Association for Supervision and Curriculum Development, 1985.

Clark, C. M., and Yinger, R. J. *The Hidden World of Teaching: Implications of Research on Teacher Planning.* East Lansing, Mich.: Michigan State University, Institute for Research on Teaching, 1980.

Cusick, P. A. *The Egalitarian Ideal and the American High School: Studies of Three Schools.* New York: Longman, 1983.

Denham, C., and Lieberman, A., eds, *Time To Learn.* Washington, D.C.: U. S. Department of Education, National Institute of Education, 1980.

Doyle, W. "Classroom Organization and Management." In *Handbook of Research on Teaching,* 3rd ed., edited by M. D. Wittrock. New York: Macmillan Co., 1986.

Giroux, H., and Penna, A. W. "Social Education in the Classroom: The Dynamics of the Hidden Curriculum." In *Curriculum and Instruction: Alternatives in Education,* edited by H. A. Giroux, A. N. Penna, and W. F. Pinar. Berkeley, Calif.: McCutchan, 1979.

Kulik, C. C., and Kulik, J. A. "Research Synthesis on Ability Grouping." *Educational Leadership* 39(1982):619-21.

Lipsitz, J. *Successful Schools for Young Adolescents*. New Brunswick, N.J.: Transaction, 1984.

Purkey, S. C., and Smith, M. S. "Effective Schools: A Review." *Elementary School Journal* 83(1983):426-52.

Rosenbaum, J. E. "Social Implications of Educational Grouping." In *Review of Research in Education*, Vol. 8, edited by D. C. Berliner. Washington, D.C.: American Educational Research Association, 1980.

Sanford, J. P. "Comparison of Heterogeneous and Homogeneous Junior High Classes." Austin, Tex.: University of Texas, Research and Development Center for Teacher Education, 1980.

Slavin, R. E. *Ability Grouping and Student Achievement in Elementary Schools: A Best-Evidence Thesis*. Report No. 1. Baltimore, Md.: Center for Research on Elementary and Middle Schools, The Johns Hopkins University, 1986.

CHAPTER 9

What Do We Mean By Quality in Education?

Jane Stallings

W HAT IS QUALITY IN EDUCATION? THERE ARE likely to be as many answers to the question as there are respondents.

When people are asked what students should learn in school, however, there is some consistency. Parents, teachers, administrators, and captains of industry usually list the following: a usable knowledge base, problem-solving skills, cooperative group skills, inquiry skills, perseverance, an appreciation of the arts, social and personal responsibility, self-respect, and respect for others.

Teachers and administrators sometimes equate quality in education with covering all the pages in a textbook by the end of the year and getting correct answers on short-answer factual tests. Of what value is having every student read every page if ideas do not come alive in such a way that students understand relationships, grasp concepts, and use the ideas in years to come?

Quality education develops meaning and connections in the minds of students. Information, questions, activities, and assignments stimulate thinking and develop problem-solving skills so that knowledge gained is usable.

Exemplifications of Quality

Quality is exemplified in the following accounts of three very different classrooms.

In an inner-city school, a teacher of literature was teaching a class of mostly black, low-achieving, junior high students. The students were all in their seats busily working when the bell rang. They were solving a riddle written on the chalkboard as the teacher took roll and passed out papers. The riddle related to the day's assignment and contrasted Langston Hughes with other authors they had studied. After a brief discussion, the teacher read aloud the Hughes poem "Mother to Son" and the students followed along. At the conclusion, the teacher asked,

"Terry, what does the author mean by the line in the poem, 'Life ain't been no crystal stair'?"

"That life has not always been perfect. There are problems sometimes," answered Terry.

"What made you think that, Terry?" asked the teacher.

"Well, the mother in the poem said her stair of life had tacks in it," responded Terry.

"Good analysis, Terry. What in the world is a tack in life? Joe?"

"Something that kind of tears you up," Joe answered.

"That's right, Joe. Have you ever had a tack in your life?"

Joe looked thoughtful and uttered softly, "When I didn't make the football team last fall."

"That was a pretty big tack, Joe, but you didn't give up. I saw you out there practicing this morning."

The teacher next introduced Hughes' short story, "Thank you, M'am," a story of a purse snatcher and an old lady. New words were explained in the context of the story and in the students' lives. At one point the teacher said, "Visualize being that old lady going home from work late at night and having someone run past and grab your purse. See it in your minds and write a few feeling words." All of the students looked pensive and then wrote: "scared, angry, tired, lonely, mad." The teacher then asked the students to read silently the next three pages to see how the old lady surprised the purse snatcher.

Focusing questions guided the students' silent reading. Student interpretations of passages were respected. At the end of the period, students wrote two paragraphs comparing "Thank you, M'am" by Hughes with a Hemingway short story read the previous week.

In a privileged private girls' school, a world history teacher had assigned each student to make an in-depth report on a critical event related to World War I. The selections for reports were made from a four-by-four grid: one axis listed the four years of the war; the other axis was defined by battles or events occurring on the eastern, southern, and western fronts, and at sea. To orient the girls to this European war, the teacher asked each girl to list the countries from which her ancestors had come. The list included almost all of the European countries.

The first report of the day was given by a girl presenting pictures and a vivid description of the events leading up to the sinking of the *Lusitania* and the impact this event had upon the United States. The teacher commented positively on the depth of the student's analysis. To involve other students, the teacher asked, "How might history have been different if the *Lusitania* had been a German ship?" A lively discussion took place among the girls. One suggested that the United States would not have entered the war. Another said the United States would have entered, but on the side of the Germans. After each remark the teacher asked the students to support their points of view through something they had read.

In a rural high school, a teacher of current events had videotaped a recent tax reform discussion involving four state and federal politicians. The students were told to think about how the tax reform would affect them and their families. The teacher gave the students a structured overview outlining the major issues of the tax reform being proposed. The students were asked to listen and record statements and points of view on each issue made by each discussant. At the end of the 12-minute tape, students were given time to analyze the issues covered and the contrasting points of view.

Next, students met in small work groups to develop a specific point of view. Students were to arrive at conclusions and collaborate on a report. The teacher provided the groups with other sources of information (e.g., newspaper and journal articles). After 20 minutes of group work, summary statements were made by each group. An argument developed regarding who would gain and who would lose if the tax reform was enacted. The discussion rules required arguments to be defended by facts. For the following week each work group was assigned to interview an adult family member, a banker, an educator, someone representing the medical profession, and the armed forces. The interview questions asked, "How do you think the tax reform will affect you and your work?" The goal of this project was to sample different points of view on a critical issue and to estimate how well-informed people seemed to be.

Characteristics of Effective Instruction

Although the students described in the classrooms above were very different in age, cultural background, and subject matter studied, the teachers were using similar instructional strategies. Many of their strategies have been identified through classroom research as effective in keeping students involved and focused on the required subject matter. Each teacher planned a variety of interesting activities for each class period which allowed the students to read, write, speak, listen, speculate, and visualize other times and places. Students who are allowed to use a variety of modalities (e.g. seeing, hearing, doing, feeling, speaking, etc.) are more likely to stay involved in their lessons and to integrate the learning into useful patterns. Structuring what is being learned through graphic organizers makes it easier to store the information in long-term memory and retrieve it as needed in new situations.

All three teachers involved their students in thought-provoking discussions. They used strategies that required all the students to think and to participate. Their comments on students' contributions were low-key, specific, and supportive.

Elements of Instructional Quality

An analysis of instruction suggests three elements of learning with useful implications for classroom teaching: (1) memory, (2) understanding, and (3) reasoning or problem solving. All three of these learning functions are necessary for students to process and use information.

Memory. Memory skills are essential for students to succeed in basic reading, writing, and computation. Ample research in the 1970s indicates that a very structured, carefully sequenced approach is effective in developing memory skills/basic skills. Rosenshine (1982) in summarizing this literature says:

In general, to the extent that students are younger, slower, and/or have little prior background, teachers are more effective when they:
- Structure the learning experience
- Proceed in small steps but at a rapid pace
- Give detailed and redundant instructions and explanations
- Use a high frequency of questions and overt, active practice
- Provide feedback and corrections, particularly in the initial stages of learning new material
- Have a success rate of 80 percent or higher in initial learning
- Divide seatwork assignments into smaller segments or devise ways to provide frequent monitoring
- Provide for continued student practice (overlearning) so that they have a success rate of 90-100 percent.

Interaction is started by the teacher presenting a small bit of information, asking a question, and calling for an individual or group response. Praise is offered if the answer is correct and correction is given if the response is incorrect.

Research on teaching conducted during the past 15 years shows that most students can, through sufficient drill and practice, memorize and be able to recall facts that are important for them for testing situations (Brophy and Good, 1974).

Understanding. In addition to facilitating student memorization of facts, instruction should also develop students' understanding of lesson content. Every student walks into the classroom with some experience and knowledge, but this prior learning differs widely, especially among children from varied socioeconomic and ethnic backgrounds. Cognitive psychologists have studied linkages between new information and prior knowledge and experience. Teachers should help students make these linkages. In effective education, teachers understand the students' culture and use examples in instruction from their background.

How the teacher structures new information influences what students will be able to link to their existing information. Calfee and Shefelbine (1981) describe the mind as a filing system of hooks or pegs on which to hang information. This filing system is the long-term memory from which information can be retrieved and used in other situations. Students need help in building these filing systems.

For information to be filed, it must first be noticed. Broadbent (1975) wrote that only some of the available information will receive attention. If this selection is not made deliberately, it will certainly be decided by chance factors. If something is not noticed at the time it happens, it has hardly any chance of affecting long-term memory. It is the teacher's role to make certain that students notice the information and make a link with existing information, thus ensuring storage in long-term memory.

As teachers help students build an information base, it is important to check for understanding. The critical nature of checking for understanding was shown in a study conducted by Webb (1980). In a group problem-solving task, those students who received an explanation after making an error solved the problems correctly on another trial. The explanation did not have to be directed toward a particular student, but toward any student within the same group. The important factor was that all students were checked for understanding and given feedback. Other students in groups that did not receive explanations after making an error were not able to solve the problems on the second trial.

Problem Solving/Reasoning. The need to train students in problem-solving or reasoning skills has been receiving increasing attention, both from the educational system and from industry. In a recent survey of electronic firms in California's Silicon Valley, business leaders were asked to identify the skills most lacking in their recently hired employees, those skills that the educational system should help students develop to become effective employees. The majority of respondents reported that schools should help students develop problem-solving skills; such skills were needed by employees at all levels (Needels, 1982). The respondents reported that many of their recently hired employees, whether high school or college graduates, were deficient in reasoning and problem-solving skills. G. H. Hanford, President of the College Board, notes that, "The decade-long decline in test scores appears largely due to the fact that reasoning ability in secondary schools is not what it used to be. In recent years, students in lower grades show marked improvement in reading, writing, and other basic skills, but students fall behind when problems get more complex." The College Board (in 1983) funded a study to identify ways reasoning and problem solving could be taught.

Inquiry methods are expected to develop problem-solving skills. Collins and Stevens (1982) identified instructional strategies of expert teachers who used inquiry methods effectively. The authors identified five strategies: (1) systematic variation of examples, (2) counter examples, (3) entrapment strategies, (4) hypothesis identification strategies, and (5) hypothesis evaluation strategies. Even though the teachers observed by Collins and Stevens taught different content areas, the authors reported the same strategies were consistently used by all the teachers. Thus the strategies are not domain-specific but can be applied to different content areas.

It is important for teachers to know the psychological processes and structures that students must develop to achieve desired behavioral objectives. Any one lesson could require drill and practice, checks for understanding, and problem solving. Teachers need an instructional repertoire, and the knowledge of which strategy is likely to develop memory, understanding, or reasoning. The focus here is not on extremes or singular points of view. Broadbent (1975), in speaking of extremes comments that:

> ... the lesson of cognitive psychology is that each of us acquires during life certain strategies of encoding the outside world, of organizing memory, and of proceeding from one step in an operation to the next, and that these may be highly general in their later use. The successful teacher, of course, has always known this, but in standing out for the middle ground between mechanical drill on the one hand and the abandonment of all positive teaching on the other, he/she can now claim the support of contemporary cognitive psychology. (p. 175)

Teacher Judgment and Expectations

All teachers make judgments about student abilities and develop a set of expectations that determine the quality of the curriculum they offer and the instructional strategies they use. In a summary of studies on teacher expectations, Brophy and Good (1974) reported that students for whom teachers held low expectations were treated less well than other students. They tended to be seated farther away from the teacher, received less eye contact, and were smiled at less often. They received less instruction, had fewer opportunities to learn new materials, and were asked to do less work. Teachers called on these students less often and tended to ask them simple rote-answer questions. They were given less time to respond and fewer probing questions or guides when their answers were wrong. They remained low-achieving students. In effective education, teachers expect the best of all students and provide opportunities for students to participate in interesting activities.

In an effort to change teacher and student perceptions of low-achieving students, Morine-Dershimer (1983) trained a group of teachers to ask higher level questions of low-achieving students. The questions elicited ideas, hunches, opinions. When students in the class were asked to check the names on a list of those who make good contributions to the class discussion, low-achieving students' names were checked as well as high-achieving students. Low-achieving students even checked their own names, indicating a sense of self-accomplishment. In a group of control classrooms, teachers were not given the special training. Low-achieving students in these classrooms were seldom involved in discussions, nor were they rated as making contributions. This point is important. If teachers do not expect that low-achieving students can take part in higher level activities and discussions, they will not give them a chance to participate. Effective education should be available to all students, offering everyone interesting and diversified ways to learn.

Planning for Different Modalities

People learn in different ways. Some consider themselves to be auditory, visual, or kinesthetic learners. But most people are multi-sensory and learn best when learning is reinforced through the use of several modalities. In an effective education, teachers plan lessons so that students may use several modalities to learn what is required. Each class period is organized so that students may listen to instruction or watch video instruction; discuss what was heard or seen; structure what was learned either in diagrams, pictures, outlines, or structured overviews; perhaps do reinforcing drill and practice; and finally do a written assignment regarding what was learned in the lesson. Students need opportunities to use eyes, ears, hands, and mouth. To learn, students must be involved. The research indicates that students are more involved and on-task in classrooms where several different activities are provided that require the use of several learning modalities (Stallings and Mohlman, 1981).

Interactive Instruction and Levels of Questions

The purpose of interactive instruction is to involve all the participants. Every time a teacher asks a question, a decision is made regarding whom to call upon. This is an important decision because it determines who will participate and who will not. For the most part, unless they consciously make an effort, teachers call upon volunteers. The effect of this practice is to limit participation and positive reinforcement to the eager, high-achieving students. The research on interaction suggests that students stay more involved and participate more in classrooms where teachers call on students by name rather than calling upon volunteers (Stallings and Mohlman, 1981). Effective teachers allow and encourage all students to participate.

When asking questions, teachers should be aware of the type of thinking they are stimulating in students. Most questions asked in classrooms require simple recall on the part of the students. For the most part, this type of question exercises the memory. Quality in education develops, in addition to memory, the thinking, reasoning, and evaluating skills of the mind through varied activities, assignments, discussions, and tests that require higher thinking.

Brainstorming or asking for students' reasoned opinions encourages a different kind of thinking. Problem-solving sessions should allow students to generate hypotheses, speculate about outcomes, plan, execute a plan, and evaluate. Even routine discussions of mathematics, literature, or social studies can be thought-producing; e.g., What do you think will happen next? What leads you to that conclusion? What is another way to arrive at a solution to that problem? Students should be encouraged to be inquisitive, to initiate questions, and to demand to understand.

Using different levels of questions is important to developing student thinking skills. If teachers do not ask questions that make students think at higher levels, it is unlikely that their thinking skills will improve. Students need a variety of questions to help them develop the skills to assess problem situations, gather information, analyze, evaluate, generate solutions, and test ideas. The types of questions asked determine the types of thinking skills required.

Recall the story of Little Red Riding Hood. What happens differently in your own thinking when you are asked the following kinds of questions?

1. Who was Red Riding Hood visiting?
2. Why did she have cookies in her basket?
3. How was Red Riding Hood like you?
4. How might the story have been different if the wolf had been an elephant?
5. Write a story from the wolf's point of view.
6. Was the woodcutter justified in killing the wolf? Why?

Even young children can answer these kinds of questions and have fun in the process. Inquiry, imagination, and creativity need time on the classroom agenda.

Conclusion

Clearly, the first charge of schools is to provide an education that develops basic skills and a substantial knowledge in content areas. But an effective education must prepare students to participate responsibly in a democratic society. The graduates of effective schools will be able to ask questions and search for answers. They will be able to compare, contrast, evaluate ideas or products, and make decisions. They will have the requisite knowledge to contribute ideas in their workplace; they will have the social and communication skills to interact productively with peers.

An education of quality awakens students to the excellence inside them and provides realistic goals for what can be accomplished in their lives. The challenging question for school administrators is: Are the students in your school receiving the elements of such an education?

References

Anderson, L.; Evertson, C.; and Brophy, J. "An Experimental Study of Effective Teaching in First-Grade Reading Groups." *Elementary School Journal* 4(1979):192-223. (ERIC No. EJ 201 788).

Broadbent, D. "Cognitive Psychology and Education." *British Journal of Educational Psychology* 45(1975):162-76.

Brophy, J., and Good, T. *Teacher-Student Relationships: Causes and Consequences.* New York: Holt, Rinehard, and Winston, 1974.

Calfee, R., and Shefelbine, J. "A Structured Model of Teaching." In *Evaluation Roles in Education*, edited by Lewey and DeNevo. New York: Gordon and Breck, 1981.

Collins, A., and Stevens, A. "Goals and Strategies of Inquiry Teachers." In *Advances in Instructional Psychology*, Vol. II, edited by R. Glaser. Hillsdale, N.J.: Lawrence Erlbaum Associates, 1982.

Hanford, G. *San Francisco Chronicle,* January 29, 1983, p. 3.

Morine-Dershimer, G. "Instructional Strategy and the Creation of Classroom Status." *AERJ* 20(1983):645-61.

Needels, M. "Industry's Willingness To Collaborate with the Education System: A Survey of California's Silicon Valley." Menlo Park, Calif.: SRI International, 1982.

Rosenshine, B. "Teaching Functions in Instructional Programs." Paper presented at the National Invitational Conference on Research in Teaching, 1982, Implications for Practice, Warrenton, Va. (ERIC No. ED 221 538).

Stallings, J. "Implementation and Child Effects of Teaching Practices in Follow Through Classrooms." *Monographs of the Society for Research in Child Development* 40(1975):50-93.

Stallings, J., and Mohlman, G. "School Policy Leadership Style, Teacher Change and Student Behavior in Eight Schools." Final report. Washington, D.C.: National Institute of Education, 1981.

Webb, N. "A Process Outcome Analysis of Learning in Group and Individual Settings." *Journal of Educational Psychology* 15(1980):69-83.

CHAPTER 10

Conclusion: What Is in Retrospect And Prospect?

Herbert J. Walberg

T HE PUBLIC HAS INCREASED EDUCATIONAL SPENDING, and considerable reforms have been achieved in the last few years. But principals still face serious problems; they are being called upon to do more at a difficult time. Can constructive reforms be sustained? Can the schools be further improved? What should be done?

It is not our purpose to answer these questions directly. The answers will be many and varied depending on local circumstances and preferences. Some ways of thinking about continuing problems and solutions, however, may be helpful and concisely stated.

The Reports in Critical Retrospect

The reform reports as a set must be flawed, if for no other reason than they disagree on what should be taught. One urges more science; another, more English; and still others, more civics and history. But there are only so many energies of mind, hours in the day, and days in the year; a balance must be struck. How can it be done?

The first principle is to follow Aristotle's advice: Consider the source. It would be surprising if the National Science Foundation placed greater priority on reading than mathematics, or if the International Reading Association called for sacrifices of reading time to do more mathematics; or if the Council on Economic Development wanted more time for the arts and music and less for basic skills and word processing. About all of the reforms, we must ask with the Greeks, whose ox is gored, and with the Romans, who benefits?

Furthermore, because of the way commissions operate, they are likely to yield statements not only of special interests but with certain predictable deficiences (Peterson, 1983):

1. The report is almost certain to exaggerate the problem it addresses.
2. The report will state only broad, general objectives.

3. The report will recommend changes beyond current technology and resources.
4. The report will not spell out the details of its proposed innovations.
5. The report will seldom call for institutional reorganization.
6. The report will poorly document the value of the solution it proposes.

From the standpoint of public policy, moreover, many also lack a "focused statement of the problem to be analyzed, methodical evaluation of existing research, reasoned consideration of options, and a presentation of supporting evidence and argumentation for well-specified proposals" (Peterson, p. 3). The current reports can be evaluated by such criteria; and those that are deficient can be discounted.

Why the Reports Are Important

Although the reports may lack balance and deserve criticism, they contain insights, facts, and values that riveted the public interest; and they were developed by prominent citizens of good will. Even if principals disagree with the reports, legislators are calling upon them to enact recommended reforms; it does little good merely to point out deficiencies.

For principals to hide their heads in the sand, or stick their feet in the mud will only alienate the public. A cooperative spirit, an extended hand, and a willingness to think seriously and act accordingly with potential partners all seem in order.

Citizens and their elected representatives are legally and financially responsible for public education. Their values largely determine what takes place in schools; their characteristics as citizens and parents provide the context for the child's education. Although principals can think with them about values and goals, it is citizens who must confront and decide about the difficult balances of excellence and equality, general and specialized education, humanities and sciences, the academic and the practical, the child and the curriculum.

Still, principals and other educators have been taught to give these matters professional and systematic consideration. Wise physicians inform patients about the costs, benefits, and risks of treatment. So too can educators ensure that important aspects of current problems and solutions are duly weighed.

If *A Nation at Risk* asserted a reasonable value judgment in encouraging more mathematics and science, the International Reading Association was also right in urging that we avoid neglecting verbal skills. If the National Commission is right in urging more time in school, then surely the quality of that time and the nature of the content also deserve consideration (Wynne and Walberg, 1984). Just as surely, educational psychologists have long warned about unduly favoring thought over feeling over behavior.

Principals, moreover, can be expected by training and experience to have a broad knowledge of the nature of society, knowledge, and learner, how these are changing, and how they are likely to change still further in the future. They can and should put this knowledge before citizens and their representatives who must choose among competing values.

And like physicians, principals and other educators have an increasing technical knowledge of means and ends, of causes and effects (Wynne and Walberg, 1984; U.S. Department of Education, 1986). The patient and the family must face the risks of expensive, dangerous, and painful operations. They decide; the physician informs and implements. Similarly, once the public decides about the curriculum and objectives, principals can best apply the growing knowledge of which means promote given ends, which instructional and other procedures are more productive in achieving given objectives.

Principals can contribute to the attainment of educational objectives because of their special and growing scientific knowledge of what works. The synthesis of thousands of studies demonstrates that some instructional procedures and techniques are far more effective than others (Wynne and Walberg, 1984). We have shown here how school time can be increased and optimized. We have indicated how the quality of instruction and parental involvement can increase learning without necessarily expending larger financial and human resources.

Principals in particular must study and evaluate the new educational reforms as they are taking place; they must learn what is working effectively and what is not. Schools need even better goal and program articulation. And research can and should be built into reform efforts. What may be most significant in the final analysis is the extent to which principals can put such ideas and research into practice.

References

Peterson, P. E. "Did the Education Commissions Say Anything?" *Brookings Review*, Winter 1983, 3-11.

U.S. Department of Education. *What Works: Research on Teaching and Learning*. Washington, D.C.: DOE, 1986.

Wynne, E.A., and Walberg, H.J., eds. *Developing Character: Transmitting Knowledge*. Posen, Ill.: ARL Press, 1984.